What's Your What?

How to Ignite Your Unique Brand

JULIE MORET

A HIGHLAND HOUSE BOOK
ISBN: 9781618685582
ISBN (eBook): 9781618685575

WHAT'S YOUR WHAT?
How to Ignite Your Unique Brand

Cover design by Christian Holihan and Lauren Gomes

To Jason, my publicist.

Also my electrician, plumber, attorney, business manager, carpenter, stylist, and best friend. Thank you for supplying me with endless fodder for my talks. Love you, Punkin.

And to Ryan, my true source of inspiration.

I love you to the moon and down again, and around the world and back again...

Contents

Foreword by

Michael Bernard Beckwith

If you're ready to unleash your inner Don Quixote to "reach the unreachable star" and "live the impossible dream," then you're primed for taking a life-changing, inspiring journey with Julie Moret. I offer one caution: Once you step firmly on the path of your life's purpose and passion, you will no longer fit back into the small space of existence you once occupied.

It was eighteen years ago that I first met Julie in a class I was teaching at the Agape International Spiritual Center, the trans-denominational spiritual community I founded in 1986. Even then, I sensed that within her lived the heart of a minister. Respecting that this was a sacred matter between Julie and Spirit, I kept my observation to myself. But it was no surprise when she eventually enrolled in Agape's ministerial school, graduated in 2009, and is now an Agape staff minister. Knowing her spirit as I do, what she offers in this book is a trustworthy path, time-tested in the laboratory of her own life experience.

A vital ingredient in Julie's equation for activating your creative self-expression is identifying what inspires you, what ignites your spirit. This can be challenging because what lights our fire is often pushed aside by limiting self-talk, fear, and excuses like: "Oh, no one in my family has ever done that and wouldn't like it if I were to step out in such a way." Or, "Oh, I'd never be successful at that and I'd end up hungry and broke." Drowning out those voices, as Julie proved in her own process, is completely possible and not as difficult as you may think. Your divine muse is sitting right within you, just waiting for that little opening in your consciousness when she can bestow Heaven's kiss of inspiration upon your receptive consciousness.

Self-expression is so vital to our self-actualization that it caused psychologist and humanistic philosopher Erich Fromm to say, "I feel that the only thing that will save civilization...is the renaissance of the spirit—a rebirth of the belief in man himself, in his essential creativeness." In my own experience, I have realized how pain pushes us until a higher vision for our life pulls us into authentic self-expression. Accepting our innate, creative nature is the key to our inner treasure house of riches. But to simply hold or place the key in the lock is not enough. We have to turn the key in order to enter the treasure house.

Once Julie committed to remaining steadfast in her own self-discovery process, she realized that it is necessary to break all agreements that have been made with mediocrity. She immediately stopped running the racket of staying small to please society, family, friends, or bosses. That was the pivotal moment when she became pulled by the vision that had always been stirring within her. Every individual has this intrinsic impulsion to live the purpose for which they have taken a human incarnation.

We energize inspiration through spiritual practices that sensitize our intuition, the receptacle of inspiration. Practices including meditation, affirmative prayer, and life visioning unite us directly to the divine mind, allowing us to catch the highest vision for our life. The great Sufi master Hazrat Inayat Khan put it this way: "It is by focusing the mind to the divine mind that man receives inspiration. One feels that one is raised from the earth when one's mind is focused on the divine mind, for inspiration comes from the divine mind."

I wholeheartedly encourage you to put into action the practices Julie teaches in *What's Your What?* By doing so, you will turn the key to the treasure house of your own inner being. And once you cross the threshold, you will stand face-to-face with the unique expression of beauty and creativity that is you, freely offering your gifts, talents, and skills to the world as no one else can.

Michael Bernard Beckwith
Founder, Agape International Spiritual Center
and author of *Life Visioning*

Acknowledgements

I am grateful for my many tribes: my family (parents, siblings, aunts, uncles, cousins, and all our many branches), friends, and the Agape International Spiritual Center community, all of whom have been steadfast guideposts on my twisty, winding, often surprising journey.

To Grandpa Loverbaby, best place in the world is right by your side holding hands.

Love to Monnae Michael, my daily phone call and genius Agape Practitioner.

To Kathleen McNamara, for friendship and counsel. Thank you for adopting Jason, Ryan, and me!

To Angie Craig, for your cool steadfastness and balanced voice of reason. It is a pleasure working/playing with you. Your presence gave me the space to write this book—still not going to karaoke with you though!

To Lauren Gomes, thank you for getting the ball rolling. We are so grateful for your time and talent!

To Adrienne Malin and Mary Miller, thank you for your editing and input. I am extremely grateful for the time and energy you devoted towards shaping this book!

To Maria Carranza, my Florida guardian angel. Thank you for getting me out into the world!

To Mark Wind and Chris Lawson with CAA. You made a dream come true and didn't even know it! Eternal gratitude!

Mary Fulginiti, Rick Genow and Hannah Mulderink from Stone, Meyer, Genow, Smelkinson & Binder, LLP (SMGSB), thank you for taking such good care of me. You all are exceptional!

To Nena, Anthony, Michael, Hannah and the folks at Highland House, thank you for believing in me. So grateful to be on this journey with you!

To Al, Woody, Gregory, Emma, Jane, Patrick, Philip, Viveca, and Marianne, thank you for lighting my path with stardust and mirroring back to me a brilliance I continue to strive toward.

My special thanks and gratitude to Michael Bernard Beckwith. All we really want in life is to be seen by someone who matters. Thank you for seeing me, and doing something about it.

Introduction

A Journey Worth Taking

You have had that moment. The moment when you feel your heart swell, every cell in your body awake with promise and excitement. You know the excellence you came into this world to live, and more than that, you know it is possible to realize your fullest potential. You feel, in that moment, that anything can happen and your heart sings with joy and anticipation. Finally, you will live the life you always knew was possible.

Then, about an hour passes. You are still pretty energized. Maybe you even planned a few steps to take in order to manifest the insights gained during your moment of inspiration. Another hour passes. It is all still great; you just need to fold the laundry first. Clean the grout around the bathtub. Pick up the kids. Watch the game. Check email. Eat. Drink. Text. Tweet. Smoke. Facebook. Whatever your old, standby way of numbing out is, this is when it tends to rear its tempting head. Thus begins the dance with our elusive friend—Inspiration. There one minute, gone the next. Quick bursts of elation and anticipation, then dropped like a hot rock or a bad date.

So why care about this seemingly fickle quality? Certainly because when it is good, it is so, so good. Inspiration can be described the way Robert G. Ingersoll described love, "...the magician, the enchanter, that changes worthless things to joy, and makes right royal kings and queens of common clay. It is the perfume of that wondrous flower, the heart, and without that sacred passion, that divine swoon, we are less than beasts; but with it, earth is Heaven, and we are gods."

Inspiration is the swell that rises up in your heart and gives you a brilliant shining glimpse of your divine nature. How then, can you learn to court and nurture this wispy treasure so that you may live more and more in that highest of highs, Divine Inspiration. This is the quest, to know what inspiration is, where it is, and how you can access it and help others do likewise. All human beings are points of inspiration. It is no longer about finding something "out there" to light you up with a jolt of inspiration like a hot shot of espresso. The mission at hand is for each person to claim his or her existence as a point of light. It is each person's obligation at birth—actually before birth—to illuminate their spot in the universe. We all come into this world with the job of inspiring life in our own unique way. What is your way? This is the worthy quest you now embark upon.

What's Your What?

In fact, take a moment right now. Take a deep breath. Exhale fully. You have picked this book up for a reason. There is something that wants to be more alive within you. Take another full, deep, easy breath. In this moment, jump into a fully awakened state. You can backfill as needed with daily spiritual practices, lessons, learnings, research—whatever it takes to maintain this level of awakened consciousness. Right now, however, choose to shift gears from any state of deficiency or incompletion and immediately propel yourself into the awareness that you are made in the image and likeness and goodness of God and that all of the wholeness, prosperity, creativity, love, joy, and perfection that exists within God, exists within you. Right now.

From this vantage point of full realization, write, in one sentence or two, who you are and why you are here. Do not take a lot of time thinking this through. This is not an intellectual pursuit. You have existed for all of eternity; your soul has easy clarity. Simply take a full deep breath. Move into the conscious awareness that everything you need, you have. There is nothing to be shy or humble about. It is not about you. You are the vehicle. The universe is fully available to you in this moment. The universe planted a seed of specialness within you. The purpose of the gift is for you to reveal it and share it. Why are you here? What is your purpose in this lifetime?

_____

_____

_____

Much, if not all, of the suffering that occurs in our world is from people who, for whatever reasons, are not living that spark of magnificence that first breathed them into life. When I am being the joy I came here to be, I do not need to spin internal soap operas around what "he did" or "she said." I do not have the time. Who has time to hijack airplanes or plant bombs when there is a sculpture screaming to be chiseled free? Ultimately, that is what this book is about. It is about freedom. Human beings are free when their minds are free, when they have the safe, nurturing space and time to be the creative, generative beings they really are, rather than Gumby drones built by fear-based news, media, and corporations.

If you viewed me from childhood, I would be the last person you would ever imagine to espouse inspiration. I began writing diaries at age seven. Almost every page written from seven to twenty-seven talked about wanting to be dead. When I was nine, I wrote a will: books to my older sister, dolls to my younger sister, and jewelry and piggy bank to my parents. At eleven, I wrote a suicide note, ate a bottle of children's aspirin, and then lay down on my bed and waited to die. I still remember my surprise when, an hour later, my mother called out for me to come to dinner. I popped up off the bed, mentally taking note that I had not, in fact, died, and ran off to supper.

What's Your What?

Somehow, even with a death wish predominant within me, even with all of the crazy death-defying behaviors of my young adulthood, such as daring myself to walk alone through Central Park in New York City at night, through all of that, there was something more. Some abiding presence, some presence like the faintest of heartbeats that let me know beyond all appearances that my life is for me. Your life is for you. It always has been. Learning to work with your indwelling inspiration is a way of self-resuscitating when life's challenges seem too much to bear.

We all have our stories about how life got derailed. For me, while radiance was one of the gifts I came into this world to share, I, like so many people, felt a need to dim myself and fly under the radar. When we do this, it is like trying to grow a seed in the dark. Eventually the life force dies off or mutates. Blanketing over your Truth does not work, and it is destructive to our planet. When you do not hold up your end, the world's energy sags. It is like being the first spot of decay on a tooth. If the tooth does not get cleaned, the decay creates a cavity. If the cavity is not tended to, a root canal is needed. If the root canal is ignored, then before you know it you are gumming your way through supper.

In a sense, this is a handbook for getting back on track and soaring in your life through a process of practical scientific reasoning and the supportive application of baby step after baby step. Most importantly, however, this is an inquiry to discover how to let your spark of inspiration carry you through to the finish line so that the thing inside of you that bursts forth periodically, that thing you know you are here to be, is fully realized in your lifetime.

Many people would like to feel what it feels like to throw themselves into a passion or conviction. Yet the society we live in does not cater toward that kind of radical individuality. How easy it is to fall prey to the soullessness that occurs in society when experiences become standardized. It is your responsibility to tend to your creativity. It is on your shoulders to ensure that you do not become ensnared in lethargy and production-line mentality. You must raise yourself up above the malaise of normalcy. Society will try to coddle you with mediocrity. It will try to keep you in nice, tight little boxes with fear-based Western medicine and nightly news broadcasts that are now no longer just nightly or news. It is up to you to chart your own course. It is up to you to hear and respond to the call inside your soul. When you do, when you become the rare individual who is willing to step forward in a bold and lively manner, you become like an exploding meteor, unfathomably brilliant. I know in my gut that this fullness of being is available to all people. It is the true nature of all people. It is your true nature.

The question is, what's your what? What are you here for? We are not generalized human beings. We come into this life with a focus. You have arrived with specific gifts, skills, talents, abilities, and inclinations. It is time to explore that spark that lives within you, identify it, and let it become your life's center point so that when life's choices and opportunities arise you can determine if they are in alignment with your central purpose or simply unnecessary distractions. This process makes decisions easier and more clear.

Over the years, I have been honored to sit opposite hundreds of clients in therapeutic counseling sessions. Through those experiences, I became humbly aware of one thing: we know. Somewhere inside ourselves, we know who we really are and why we are really here. The frustrating truth is that while most people know who they are, all too often they spend years, sometimes a lifetime, looking all around the glaringly obvious, trying to find something that makes more sense, fits in better, is more practical, less scary, or easier to explain to Mom and Dad.

A few years ago, I was in a workshop and I was paired up with a young man who was lost. He did not know where to work, where to live, or what to do. My then-enabling self dove right in with him. We wallowed around in his hot mess all afternoon. He brought out my inner-Jewish mamma, "Oh, my goodness, we have to get you a job! We have to get you some food! What are we going to do with you?" At one point, he said that he might be able to get a job at an auto mechanic shop. I said, "Great, do you know anything about cars?" He said, "No." It was not a pretty situation. We were like two drowning people grasping after rocks as life preservers!

Finally, the workshop came to an end and I could not wait to get out of there. As I raced for the door, I overheard a surprising piece of information. I found out that the young guy I was partnered with had been tapped by a world-renowned psychic. The psychic had seen in him the extraordinary gift of intuition and had told the young man to get business cards made up. That is all he needed to do. Get business cards and the psychic would send him all of the people he did not have time to see in a day.

Now, this psychic charges $300 per hour. He was hand delivering on a silver platter a phenomenal livelihood to the young guy, but this man had no paradigm for that level of success. All he could focus on was a job, a J.O.B.—Just Over Broke. He was focused on the kind of job where people clock in and clock out for years on end until they die. He had no awareness in his consciousness that he could spend his days using his unique God-given gift as a source of nurturance, healing, and inspiration, and be lavishly, financially funded in return. It is a crime that he did not know this was possible. It is a crime not to know that about ourselves, and it happens all too often. So, this book is about allowing yourself to be the brilliance you know that you are.

We will begin by exploring what inspiration is, how it is naturally, biologically, physically, and psychologically encoded within you, and then take it home with concrete tools and resources for activating inspiration in your daily life. Keep a pen handy; there will be ample opportunity to receive insights and inspiration. As you anchor your experiential understandings by writing them down in the spaces provided, you imprint each new awareness upon your consciousness. By raising your thoughts and beliefs, you will find that the people, places, and circumstances of your life have to recalibrate themselves in order to meet you where you now choose to live.

Welcome to a journey worth taking!

1

Inspiration: Everyone Wants It, But What Actually Is It?

My teacher, Michael Bernard Beckwith, founder and spiritual director of the Agape International Spiritual Center, once spoke of the need for us to slow down long enough for our little self, our egotistical, wanting, striving, grasping, self, to catch up with our big Self, the aspect that is connected with the absolute source that is God. Slow down long enough to tune out external chatter, expectations, stresses, and pressures, and tune in to Truth, the voice within that is ever present if we will but listen. When you take that daily moment to stop, rest, and listen, then you hear, clear as a crystal bell, the clean call of your heart's desire and even more, you are fed nectar from the divine and given inspiration's holy sustenance to guide your way.

Stop right now. Take a moment and imagine plugging yourself in to the biggest power source imaginable. Take a full deep breath. Open to your connection with God, Spirit, Nature, Higher Consciousness—use whatever word works for you to describe that Supreme Source that is omnipresent—always present—in your life. You may easily feel this connection, or you may need to imagine it at first until it becomes more certain for you. Feel within yourself a sense of "all systems go," full flow between you and your higher self. Gain the sense that your source exists within you. You are, now and always, fully connected with Spirit. Take a few more full deep breaths. Now ask for guidance, support, wisdom, peace, whatever quality you most desire in this moment. Ask that you be filled with that quality. Breathe it in. Breathe in love, joy, prosperity, and wholeness. Allow yourself to be infused with the quality that is most wanting to fill you right now. Your subconscious mind cannot discern the difference between a real event or an imagined event, so give yourself what you want and then notice as your physical body produces hormones and secretes endorphins in support of this elevated state.

As you contemplate how vital it is to be intentional and conscious, ask for and receive the quality you most desire. If that quality has a color, sound, feel, or smell to it, imagine it filling you. Next, ask for guidance. Whatever is important and supportive for you right now. Breathe and allow your message to come through. You may feel that you are making it up; that is okay. Your subconscious mind functions with volition, it will give you what you need. With earnestness, ask, 'Dear God, what is my message for this day? What is most useful for me to know at this time?'

_____

_____

_____

_____

Now take a moment of gratitude for your ability to receive guidance and shift your psychological state at will. When you take the time to say thank you, you send a clear message that you are available for guidance. Even if you feel you did not receive much this time, still, the act of expressing gratitude charts a course in consciousness. It shows that receiving inspiration is the direction you choose to travel. As you do this regularly, you will find more and more that your inspiration comes when you call.

There is much talk of inspiration, yet, what actually is it? Swami Rama Tirtha delivered his lecture, "The Nature of Inspiration," at the Golden Gate Hall in San Francisco in 1903. He began by addressing the audience as, "My own Self in the form of ladies and gentlemen," and continued by telling the story of a caged parrot, which symbolized an enslaved person. He declared that there was only one true way to freedom; the "way to realization is apparent death, that and nothing else, crucifixion and nothing less, there is no other way to inspiration."

In the story, the parrot pretended to be dead and so his captors left the cage door open and he flew to freedom. Tirtha's message is that the way to realization is in getting above the body, rising to the state of inner salvation where the body is, as it were, dead. You rise to that place where the small personality is unconscious, is altogether lost, entirely left behind; that is the way to life.

> *"The very moment inspiration is there, the idea of 'I know' and 'I do it' is absent. It cannot be there... When you are playing the part of the greatest artist, there in the eyes of others, you are a great artist, but from your own standpoint you are not. No thought of 'I am doing' is present. You have become one with the All... This is the nature, the secret of inspiration."*

Inspiration, then, comes from immersion. It comes from diving so deeply into your passion that the "end goal," be it fame, money, or compliments, all of it disappears and there is only resonance between you and that thing for which you were born. Swami Rama Tirtha continued by saying,

> *"Like the bees, artists must put their lives into the sting they give. There is the whole secret of inspiration. The bee, when it stings you, dies after it. So he is inspired who gives his whole life into the sting he gives... You cannot be inspired and at the same time be an enjoyer; try to enjoy a thing and you are no longer inspired; others will*

> *enjoy you, the world will enjoy you, when you are*
> *inspired, but you yourself will not be an enjoyer*
> *and an inspired man (or woman) at the same time.*
> *You will be no enjoyer, but you will be better still,*
> *joy itself."*

This brings in a tricky component of inspiration. Once you get it and learn to invite it into your life on a regular basis, how do you keep it pure? How do you allow yourself to soar with the angels and become brilliantly radiant without getting seduced into believing that it is you, rather than God's magnificence being channeled through you? How many celebrities have we witnessed who truly held a heavenly gift and yet the moment they believed it was them, their ego self, all began to unravel?

Tirtha reminds us of this saying, "When you are above this 'I am doing, I am enjoying,' God is working through you and you are inspired; but as soon as you do a thing and accept people's reviews and favorable criticisms, people's applause, and people's flattery, the power goes out immediately. Immediately it goes out; you are brought into the cage again. Go out of the cage and you are inspired, go into the cage again and you are no more." It is time now to get out of the cage, is it not?!

It seems I have spent most of my life in a cage, captive to other's thoughts of me, held prisoner by a gaze. Does he like me? Is she disapproving of me? There is a kind of acculturated hyper vigilance, a constant "on guard" behavior that is unspoken yet taught in our earliest years. There are rules about caring what others think and striving to fit in, to not make waves. This stifling behavior poisons dreams and is certain death for creativity.

Yet, from every angle—media, society, teachers, parents, friends—the shackles of appropriateness stand at the ready, cuffing our need for expression, choking individuality. Deciding to live fully means moving forward anyway. It is the child who decides to shine anyway, even when her radiance is a constant reminder to her parents of their failures. Choosing to shine anyway means breaking unspoken contracts between lovers lulled into mediocrity. Shining your light anyway means that when you are young, other kids may call you a freak out of their own insecurity and ignorance, and when you are an adult, other adults will do the same thing just using bigger words and thicker veils of false politeness. It means traditional religious communities may be offended by your existence. It means trusting in your excellence even when you have given the performance of a lifetime and someone walks past pretending not to see you or acknowledge your exceptional art. It means blessing them and the fear and inadequacy they must feel in order to behave that way. It means knowing yourself, trusting yourself, choosing yourself, and being your own mighty champion, come what may.

Some years ago, I worked at a company where the person in charge saw my gifts and was grateful to have me on board. While most people were quite lovely to me, there was one person who did not like me. We did not know each other well, and intellectually I knew that I must remind her of someone from an earlier time in her life, a friend or sister she may have struggled with. I knew that her dislike of me was not about me. I knew that logically, but her coldness was paralyzing. For most of my life when I felt that kind of competition or judgment, I took off. I had lived as a professional leaver. The pain of another's dislike was too much for my sensitive, empathic nature.

Finally, after one too many times experiencing the violence of being ignored, I packed my bags. I was ready to run away and never come back as I had done so many times in my life. This is where spiritual maturity comes in. This is when, at last, you decide to let the pull of your soul become more important and more necessary than a disapproving glance or a rude rebuff. Are you there yet? Have you reached that boiling point of no return yet, where nobody, no way, no how will ever derail you again? Are you fed up enough? Are you hungry enough? Is the sweetness of your bliss more seductive than the bitterness of someone else who cannot deal with your brilliance?

You will walk many fine lines as you embrace your greatness. On one hand, you must stay mindful of the fact that you are a custodian of brilliance. Your greatness is not from your ego self; it is a born mandate from life. On the other hand, you are to honor this jewel and raise it up, do everything within your power to spark the most radiance possible, deterred by no one, derailed by nothing. Spiritual practices will help you stay grounded and plugged into an awareness of your true source.

It is also comforting to know that you are not alone on this journey. Humanity's current stage of evolution involves a collective embracing and embodiment of our individual life purposes. As a whole, we are no longer strictly survival based. Most do not wake each day needing to go out and hunt and forage for their day's sustenance. Most do not need to spend their waking hours struggling for the next night's shelter or fighting off wild beasts. In this way, we are both more freed up and more responsible to take our energies to the next level and move from surviving to thriving consciousness. As you enter this realm, your very presence heals and nurtures the planet.

We, as the human race, are on a learning curve. Humanity's soul lesson for the past few decades dealt with manifestation. Many learned, perhaps too well, how to amass "stuff," material goods, largely to the extent of becoming a culture of fat, soft, hoarders. What is left? What is the new direction? Is there something that satisfies more than an overly stuffed closet or a bulging belly? Yes. Certainly, the answer is yes. We are learning to fill ourselves up from the inside. We are learning to unclutter and feel satisfied through our creativity and the expression of our gifts, skills, talents, and abilities. We are learning to experience satisfaction in giving, sharing, and serving. We are learning this because we have to, because the "me/mine" mentality is imploding on us. The more globalized society becomes, the more critical it is to think holistically.

The opportunity here is to gain freedom by embodying that which you desire rather than buying it. Be it. Whatever it is that you most desire for yourself, for your family, your community, the world that you live in—whatever it is that you desire most, it is time to become the thing itself. Be the presence of peace. Be the embodiment of love, joy, happiness, prosperity, justice, freedom, and kindness.

What's Your What?

Rather than externally striving for things to create the emotions you desire to feel, use your consciousness to become what you want without having to amass the stuff society says you need in order to outwardly be who you inwardly already are! Use your mind to be joy, love, prosperity, peace, wholeness, creativity—whatever you desire. A new era is dawning, and you will see that it relies on internal technologies far more than external cravings.

Take a quality infusion break. Go back to the breath. Full, deep breathing. Become aware of the quality you desire to infuse your life with right now. Breathe it in. Breathe in whatever you desire. You are powerful beyond measure. Be filled with that quality. Let your DNA take a snap shot of this quality-infused state so that it may now replicate and magnetize people, places, and events that are congruent with this new information. I am _____. (Fill in the quality you now claim.) Say it again, I am _____. Yes, now let it be so!

In being that which you most desire, you inspire good in others as well. This is the necessary second piece. True, you are a unique, special emanation of God. But so is your neighbor, be it the person standing in a grocery store line in front of you, driving a car behind you, or someone on the other side of the world whose beliefs and philosophies make no sense to you. All are unique, necessary emanations of God. When we understand this, when we accept this, when we allow this, then will be the grand up-leveling of humanity. This will be the difference that made the difference and allowed our life form to consciously evolve and gain real, meaningful freedom.

I take this moment to rise up and stand for heightened, responsible consciousness. I stand in gratitude for myself and all those this day that have the freedom to devote time and energy toward consciously up-leveling their lives and focusing on the full expression of their life's purpose. I am grateful for those that wake this day and are unburdened with the struggles of finding shelter before nightfall or enough food to fill their bellies, and I bless those that have the ability this day to sit in meditation and receive spiritual sustenance. I bless those that have enough clean water and fresh food that they may now focus their energies toward personal transformation and being a beneficial presence on the planet. I bless your willingness to grow and stretch and become more of who you really are. How good it is to declare that we who have enough this day wear a mantle of responsibility to elevate our consciousness so that we may create a kinder, more loving, accepting home for all of humanity. Amen.

2

Inspiration Is Within:
A Closer Look at the Nature
of Inspiration

Inspiration is significantly influenced by psychologically induced flow states. Psychologist Mihaly Csikszentmihalyi's well-known studies on optimal experience revealed that what makes an experience genuinely satisfying is a state of consciousness called flow. During flow, people typically experience deep enjoyment, creativity, and a total involvement with life. Sounds good, yes? Imagine being totally involved in your own life!

In his book, *Flow: The Psychology of Optimal Experience*, Csikszentmihalyi demonstrates the ways this positive state can be controlled rather than left to chance. He teaches that, by ordering the information that enters your consciousness, you can discover true happiness and greatly improve the quality of your life. Being in a flow state, also known as being "in the zone," is an example of being in a true state of inspiration. As Tirtha noted, this flow state, which is an inspired state of action, is observable. It is palpable to those on the outside and in the witnessing of it, a feeling tone response of like kind is drawn forth from the observer.

Rosamond E.M. Harding further defined the necessary keys to inspiration in her book, *An Anatomy of Inspiration*. Harding stated that daydreaming and creative thinking are required preparatory activities for inspiration. Harding's theory helped clarify a period of my life, which I have fondly termed, "the witch years." Looking back, I realize that since childhood I had a natural proclivity for daydreaming. When there was something that interested me, or that I desired, I found myself naturally, compulsively fantasizing about it.

As a child, I was clear that this was how life worked—have a dream, desire, or want, give it energy, and it grows. The "witch years" occurred in my early twenties. Over a span of about three years, I had dozens of dramatic, immediate, intimate experiences of manifestation all arising from the practice of daydreaming, which Harding referred to as a vital component in unleashing inspiration.

During that time, I met dozens of "A-list" celebrities, a president, world-renowned singers, and great artists. My long-time fantasy of becoming a goodwill ambassador and working globally as a mediator for peace was massively engaged when I had the Forrest Gump-like experience of attending two private, black tie events at the United Nations. I dined with major world leaders and celebrities including

What's Your What?

Ted Turner, Jane Fonda, and Henry Kissinger. Many of these stories will be relayed in later chapters simply to express the sheer joy of how life works when we work it, and how inspiration is the key to igniting all manner of wonder-filled, joyous experiences.

One of my dearest experiences of inspired manifestation occurred after watching a favorite movie of mine. I had been home flipping through television stations when the film *Dirty Dancing* came on. I remembered how much I loved the movie and how captivated I was by Patrick Swayze's performance. Over the next few days, I found myself drifting in a familiar state of reverie. As a child, my mother often described me as living in a fantasy world. She said I was a "do it yourself kid," in that I would sit alone in my room for hours lost in imaginary worlds. I now understand that my drifting was not an idle pastime. Those dreamy hours were highly creative. Creation is born of thought backed by emotion. Those early years were the brewing years, the years of constructing in consciousness all of the good that is now materializing in my life.

I was in this day dreamy state, replaying highlights from *Dirty Dancing* in my mind, while working my shift as manager of an exclusive health club on West 57th Street in Manhattan. At the end of the night, just as I was closing down the club, who shows up? Patrick Swayze, the star of *Dirty Dancing*! He said he was in town while his wife performed on Broadway and since he had an injured knee, he wondered if he could come by in the evenings around closing time and soak his knee in the hot tub. What followed was about six weeks of poolside chats. I was invited to see his wife perform on Broadway and we came to realize that he and his mother had regularly purchased costumes and dancewear from my grandfather's costume store in Texas! It was a rich, sweet time that I will always cherish.

This is the life you are living, ripe with happy possibilities because, truly, you are at the helm of your experiences. You are powerful beyond measure. The key is your consciousness backed by purposeful emotion. You have the ability to self-inspire and then revel in all of the good that flows to you.

Along with promoting daydreaming, Harding also acknowledged that the appearance of inspiration is usually sudden and begins with an idea that then gets fueled by emotion. This fits well with an equation I used to post during seminars: Thought + Emotion = Creation. Inspiration is creative. It is the beginning movement in a torrential sea of unfolding wonder.

It is beneficial to take a moment and discern the difference between divine inspiration and motivation. *Wikipedia.com* defines inspiration as "sudden creativity; an uncovering or disclosure of something hidden via communication from the divine." The *Merriam-Webster Online Dictionary* calls inspiration an "arousal of the mind to special unusual activity or creativity, divine guidance, arousing to a particular emotion or action; inhalation, the act of drawing in, a psychic state to which one becomes susceptible to creative spiritual influence, or, to a varying degree, unwittingly lends oneself as an instrument for through-flowing ideas." Finally, the *American Heritage Dictionary* says inspiration is "the action or power of moving the intellect or emotions...stimulation of the mind or emotions to a high level of feeling or activity; an agency, such as a person or work of art that moves the intellect or emotions or prompts action or invention."

Inspiration has a vastly different feeling tone than motivation. Wikipedia.com defines motivation as "the set of reasons that determine one to engage in a particular behavior... motivation may be rooted in the basic need to minimize physical pain and maximize pleasure, or it may include specific needs such as eating and resting..." The *Merriam Webster Online Dictionary* describes it as "the act or process of creating incentive and drive," while the *Free Dictionary* by Farlex, calls motivation the "psychological feature that arouses an organism to action toward a desired goal... something that people do or cause to happen."

The distinction here is that motivation is something you do, force, manipulate, or make happen. It has a lower, more externally driven vibrational level than true inspiration. While motivation is useful in its own right, it does not have the same organic, spiritual nature of our indwelling inspiration. Motivation is more survival oriented or geared toward satiating the senses and winning. True inspiration simply is; inspiration bursts forth because it has to, because there is an internal need to shine. Like the tiny weed that somehow, against all odds, manages to sprout through a crack in a busy city sidewalk. The seed of you, of who you really are, is constantly striving toward full realization.

Aristotle spoke to this understanding in his telos theory in which it is understood that the oak tree already resides within the acorn.

Everything you need, want, and desire for your total fulfillment in this lifetime is already within you. Your self-inspiring self cannot help but pop up like a happy little gremlin from time to time beckoning you on, guiding you forth to your fullest, most brilliant expression.

By opening this book, you have accepted an invitation home. This is not a sweet, simple invite to which one quickly opens and RSVPs in the affirmative. You are dabbling with something far more dangerous. You are entering something like Robert Frost's description of the northern coast of California, "It looked as if a night of dark intent was coming, and not only a night, an age. Someone had better be prepared for rage." By turning these pages, you unlock the doors of passion and intensity of which Frost spoke. You are churning the caldron, unleashing the force within you, your own inborn source of inspiration that functions, as a lighthouse guiding you home unto yourself, if you will but let it.

How close can you get in this lifetime to being a fully manifested expression of God-consciousness? What places in your life want to become more free? Now is the moment to discover your indwelling inspiration and dance with it so that your inspiration becomes an internal honing device, vectoring you home unto yourself.

3

Your Biologically Encoded Good

More and more of nature's laws are constantly being discovered. As the profundity of our unfolding awareness continues, can there be any doubt that Absolute Inspiration exists within the smallest neutron all the way to the grandest galaxy? Let us be reminded of the definition of inspiration: sudden creativity; an uncovering or disclosure of something hidden, a heightened feeling or activity that moves the intellect or emotions or prompts action or invention. Is this not the story of creation? Beginning with a sea of primordial soup, there came a spark, a high-level feeling, plus activity that pushed the waters about, prompting an outrageous, unfathomable invention: the birth of life. When vegetation, animals, and man all took form, were these not un-coverings or disclosures of that which was hidden yet existing as potential good?

Michael Bernard Beckwith teaches that the phrase, "In the beginning," from scripture is not speaking of an actual time when there was a beginning. Rather, it is referring to an infinite idea coming into expression. The way a seed once planted then grows into fruition. Your nature is infinite and you have a biologically encoded drive to continuously bring it to fulfillment.

Biology is the scientific study of living organisms. Based upon our definition of inspiration, sudden moments of creation, the development and genius behind all living organisms can be nothing short of pure inspiration. You are born from inspiration. Absolute Inspiration united your cells and compiled them in such a way that there is a hand and a foot and a heart and a nose that knows to sneeze out that which no longer serves. Inspiration is the primary ingredient that caused alchemical reactions to push and shove and join one cell to another forming the intricate, precise masterpiece known as your body. We are not random creations. We were not linearly devised after a series of research focus groups determined which form would be most advantageous for organelles to combine in. You were not assembled factory style, part by part, piece by piece. Inspiration happened and you were born. You are the literal embodiment of inspiration. You are inspiration materialized.

Should you ever doubt this truth, just look yourself square in the mirror and declare, "I have the genius of a herring gull!" Nobel Prize winning scientist, Albert Szent-Gyorgyi, studied herring gulls for a living. (If you think you had a hard time explaining to your mom and dad that you wanted to be an artist, imagine that dinner table conversation: "Mom, Dad, I have decided to devote my life to herring gulls!") Through his research, Szent-Gyorgyi discovered that momma gull has a red patch on her beak. At birth, baby gull knows to tap on momma gull's red patch in order to elicit a regurgitation reflex so baby can get food. Sounds simple, right? However, this grossly intricate process involves a whole series of complicated biological chain reactions with the complex underlying nervous mechanism of both momma and baby gull. For this whole interaction to work, Szent-Gyorgyi stated that it all had to develop simultaneously, which is a random mutation with zero probability. The only way he could explain this occurrence was with the concept of syntropy.

Syntropy is the opposite of entropy. Entropy is what society has bought into—a person is born, they wither, and then they die. Syntropy says that there is an innate drive within all living matter to perfect itself. You have a biologically-encoded impulse to move toward absolute fulfillment in your lifetime. There is a need that lives within you. It courses through your veins. It is imprinted within your DNA. It resides in all the spaces, and the spaces between the spaces, within your body. It is your innate desire to move toward wholeness and full realization in your lifetime. Not only do you enter this life on a dream with the seed of your greatness planted within, you enter with your own syntropic "app", an internal GPS system constantly directing and redirecting you back toward wholeness and expansion.

While there are an infinite number of examples of the inspiration that moves through animal and plant life in both simple and complex ways, we are living in a time in which we can eye witness

Absolute Inspiration sparking creation beyond planned cognition. Biology is not merely a muse for creativity. Inherent in the biology of life is inspirational potential, which must be unleashed, just like the bees who give their all in each sting. Science now understands that at your most foundational level, you have a biologically-encoded need to give everything you have to fully realize your purpose.

As we embrace this truth, we must remember that it is our total self that wants full realization, not just our intellectual minds. In his film, *"Walking Between the Worlds,"* New York Times best-selling author Gregg Braden says that our external inventions, the development of our technology and computers, are reflections of who we are internally. The computer that you use and the automated checkout line at the grocery store are external representations of your biological self. We must stay wise to what Braden knows, that our fancy technology and, oh-so-smart phones are outwardly manifested forms of our internal capabilities. Truly, the day is coming when we will tap into our brains the way we tap, tap, tap upon our keypads, and find that the data of the universe resides within, ready in all moments for your willingness to download.

How easy it is to dismiss the past while shining a spotlight on our technologically governed present, but the history of humanity's unfolding drama must not shut out our ancestors. Time and advancement are always progressing. Let us be humbled here. Let us be alerted. We must keep an awareness close to our hearts that the ancient ones descend our conscience to us. We inherit from them our own moral compass based on their trials and triumphs. We must not allow them to sink unremembered into the architecture of time. We must not draw the curtain on our ancient world, the mystics, sages, wise ones in all cultures from all times, for they are the soul of us and our thriving depends on un-tethered veils flowing freely between the past and the present. It is the creak in our bones that reminds us that we have lived and, hopefully, learned. When we mow over a past to lay new lawn for a spiffier, more efficient future, we are doomed. We stand on the brink of unprecedented technological intelligence. Be grateful for these advancements, yes, and realize that they must stay coupled with true, gut wisdom and intuition, not just tech smarts.

And so from our rapid-fire cyber growth and resultant dependency on external knowledge sources, gently now allow life to guide you back to the soul of your nature, to that place that breathes truth without needing a chart, graph, or Google search. Return home to that place that values feelings and intuition as vital technologies. Braden got it right when he said we are the thing itself. You are the thing itself. Even now, Absolute Inspiration is at hand guiding you home unto yourself, unto the feeling conviction that you are the thing itself. Everything you need, you have. Take a moment to breathe in this truth, and let it be so.

In this quiet moment, call upon the wisdom of the ages. Welcome the wise ones, the sages, the beings of support that are always around you. Without thought, simply ask for soul guidance and notice who shows up. I have a client who works in upper management at a top Fortune 500 company. When she asks for guidance, an image of Glenda the Good Witch from *the Wizard of Oz* appears. It does not matter whether it is wishful thinking on her part or a true angelic being that watches over her from the spirit world. What matters is that she has someone to call upon when she needs comforting, soothing, guidance, or protection. When she has had an especially challenging day interfacing with CFOs from major corporations, it means everything to be able to go home and imagine cuddling up in Glenda's arms—giving herself the experience of being held, nourished, and restored so she can go back out in the world the next day and run with the wolves once again.

I have a handful of guides that come to me depending on what areas I am working on. It feels wonderfully supportive to call in different beings, or archetypes to help me negotiate the various "Everests" of my day. We will discuss the role archetypes play with respect to inspiration in a later chapter. For now, simply take a few quiet moments to yourself. You may want to sit in nature or play meditative music. Become still and begin with gratitude for those who have walked before you. Become grateful for their well-earned wisdom, and ask for them to share what is most helpful for you to know this day. You may get an image, picture, feeling tone, direct knowing, word, or symbol. Receive what comes to you and take notes:

_____

_____

_____

_____

Yes, it may feel like you are making it up, but your subconscious mind is not misguided or whimsical. You get what you need. Also, this process is a practice. It is like building a muscle. As you develop a regular practice of asking and opening to guidance, you become stronger in your ability to receive clear counsel from your inner knowing. Dear Ones, guide me this day. Where shall I place my attention? What is for me this day? What am I for this day? In gratitude, I receive your guidance now. Thank you.

_____

_____

_____

_____

Consider that within your body there is an innate, ongoing drive for self-perfection. If we refer back to the part of our definition of inspiration that says, "An agency that moves the intellect or emotions or prompts action or invention," then perhaps there is a biological component which houses inspiration. Science has not yet discerned the location of syntropy. It could be localized in the hypothalamus or the pituitary, or it could be a whole body dissemination born into each cell of the nervous system, which is also known as the body's other brain. This concept of the nervous system functioning like a brain implies full-body thinking. Imagine having a full body capacity to consciously think inspiration into an awakened, active state at any moment, in any place in your body. If you have a stomachache, for example, you could "think" into that area and cure it with the healing wholeness of pure inspiration. You can literally inspire your own health.

The human urge toward syntropy is equivalent to your inborn capacity to swell with inspiration. There is something internal, perhaps cellular, which drives and awakens and desires the best of you. It functions throughout your entire body. As science advances, perhaps a time will come when people can get syntropy bypass surgery if they are feeling a blockage to their good, or syntropy replacement therapy as they age to help refresh their drive. Silly or exciting as these possibilities may be, the good news is that we do not have to wait for scientists to prove what you can know right now in your gut. There is something inside of you. It drives you. It propels you. It never gives up on you. It may rest or seem to sleep, but that is only a kindness of waiting for your readiness. This source, be it syntropy, inspiration, or God, is not an external event. It is your indwelling syntropic impulse, an innate, acculturated need to self-perfect. We have it as individuals and we have it as a people. All peoples do. It is part of man's biologically encoded good. It is the gift placed inside your soul as you slipped back into human form to dance this dance on earth once more.

I bless this Source within me. I bow in gratitude and appreciation. How many times did I believe all was lost, opportunities passed, only to learn that the abiding innocence of my Good has gently kept pace with me. As I turn toward the light of God, my heartbeat of inspiration quickens once again and I know that truly all is well. I am absolute inspiration in motion. My life is absolute inspiration in motion. This day I dive deeply into the well of infinite potentiality and resurface, like Poseidon, God of the sea, turning that which was "no-thing" into my life's fully manifested good.

4

Your Physiologically
Encoded Good

Inspiration means to draw in, as in to inhale. What a thrilling notion. Twenty-four hours a day, seven days a week, human beings involuntarily breathe in. We are automatically self-inspiring beings. Consider the sound of that statement. You are, whether you mean to or not, automatically and constantly in the process of inspiring every cell in your body. Imagine what your life would feel like if you took that intention into your every breath.

With every inhalation, I stand in dominion over my own source of inspiration. With every inhalation, I choose the breath of God. I choose the life of God. Breathing in, I am awake. I am alive. I am here. I am now. I allow myself to be awestruck by this moment, and this one...and this one...

Imagine how your life would up-level if you backed your regular common breaths with the powerful intention to reveal more and more of who you really are with each breath you take! I have a girlfriend who is currently not in a relationship though she says she would like to be. She regularly calls me to let me know about the disaster zone that is her love life. After each blind date she says the same thing, "I'm not blown away." To which I always reply, "Blow yourself away." If you want to be blown away, move to Kansas. If you want a long-term loving, monogamous relationship, take responsibility for being that. Be the earth-shattering stars and fireworks that you want to feel. When you "be it", you see it! You see the radiance in everyone around you and you attract people who are ready and willing to shine along with you.

American author and poet, Dr. Maya Angelou spoke poignantly about letting your eyes light up when you see your child. You can do that. You can decide through your actions and behaviors, to "light up" when you see your child, partner, friend, fellow driver on the freeway, grocery checkout clerk, or mail person. You can choose to become fully present and consciously see the magnificence in them. Try this as an activity, set a reminder so that just before your beloved walks in the door at night or your child comes home from school, or you set out to be with people, a ring tone reminds you to consciously "turn on."

You will be amazed at how your energy can shift a room. This is a tool that you have within you. Show up being that which you desire.

What's Your What?

Show up knowing the best of those around you, and watch how the world now has to shift, adjust, and recalibrate itself to meet you where you choose to live. Howard Thurman referred to this as "upstairs thinking." It is time to go upstairs! Choose physical actions that spark lightning bolts of inspiration within you and create domino blasts of aliveness in those around you.

Test this theory out. The next time you see someone, dear friend, beloved, or stranger, see them fully. Become totally present, cell phone off, no distractions, but more than this, bring it. Bring the quality you want to experience to that meeting. Qualities of God are things like: peace, joy, love, integrity, harmony, balance, ease, prosperity, abundance, creativity, justice, faith, and truth. See the quality you want to experience in the other person, find it in yourself, beam it, and be it. The whole interaction will be up-leveled. Yes, the other person may look at you a little strange and wonder if you have more than tea in your teacup, but this is the kind of action that our lives call for and the world is crying out for. We cannot wait for others to set the pace of our hearts and emotions. We must find ways to extract ourselves from the day-to-day malaise and be that which we desire. Your conscious physicality is another source of inspiration that is readily accessible to you.

Inspiration is indwelling. You have a reserve of greatness within you. This is why, so often, people see an artist or athlete perform brilliantly and automatically think to themselves, "I can do that." The reason we say this is because when someone allows themself to shine unabashedly, we can see and feel and hear the inspiration radiating from their body and the vibration of brilliance ping-pongs off of our own brilliance. In an instant, we are woken from lethargy and normalcy and awakened to our true nature. It is no wonder that spectator sports are such big business. Fans become identified with players, often yelling and screaming at their television sets, trying to tell the players what to do or, more likely, what they are doing wrong!

In this way, fans remotely access greatness by personalizing someone else's. The subconscious mind, which cannot discern the difference between a real event or an imagined one, then feels satisfied that the fan is living his greatness. This creates a malaise in the spectator, a lack of drive because their syntropic urge is being met externally. We want to realize our own greatness. Sure, it is great to enjoy sports and celebrate the achievements of others, but we must do so in a way that awakens our own purpose and sends us back into our life reinvigorated and energized to reveal more of ourselves.

Conversely, perhaps the rage of reality television that currently dominates the airwaves is a reflection of an unspoken societal pact to lull us into mediocrity. How empowering and rejuvenating it would be for the media to move out of reflecting normalcy and ignorance and rise into a return of portraying mythological figures such as Xena the Princess Warrior, Athena, Hercules, and Zeus. Imagine how society would shift if our daily cues from television were acts of great strength, unprecedented courage, vows of honor, heroic feats and stands for justice. If your current life structure is not gushing with physical reminders of who you really are, chapter 5 ("Go With the Flow: Your Psychologically Inspired Self") will support you in creating high level personal fulfillment by juicing your environment with conducive daily reflections of your most fully-realized self.

For now, welcome the knowledge that physically you are self-inspiring every second via your breath, and perhaps even your blood. In the classical world, one of the models offered for inspiration came from the *Problemata*. Although the author is unknown, this piece is from the peripatetic school, which followed Aristotle's teachings. The *Problemata* suggests that imbalances in the four humours are the origin of inspiration. According to this theory, inspiration physically dwells in the coursing blood that flows through your veins!

Whether it is due to inspiration coursing through great performers' and athletes' veins or energetically emanating from them, you cannot help but feel the snap, crackle, pop, of your own inspiration flooding every capillary in your body as they allow themselves to go the full distance of their physiologically inspired selves. In that moment, you have reawakened to your organic indwelling inspiration. It may out-picture as a feeling that you can do what they do, which may be true; but most importantly, it is in that moment of inspiration that you can sink deeper and open wider to God's vision for your particular life. If you allow yourself to get still, you can receive enormous insights regarding the specific brand of light you came into this world to shine.

Inspiration is within, and you have been gifted with an internal alarm clock that chimes a reminder to you approximately twelve to twenty times a minute as you regularly "self-inspire" —draw in your life's breath. It is interesting to note how the number of breaths people breathe per minute changes as humans age. Newborns breathe in approximately forty-four times per minute. Infants take in between twenty to forty breaths per minute, while preschool children slow down to twenty to thirty breaths per minute. Older children take in sixteen to twenty-five breaths per minute. Adults have the lowest rate of inhalation taking in only twelve to twenty breaths per minute. If inspiration means to take in, or breathe in, then at birth we are naturally more "inspired" and we become less so as we age.

Many would say this is part of the status quo aging process. I say, you are bound by nothing in this life. No preexisting statistic binds you to what is possible in your human experience. For example, when athletes are in their flow state, demonstrating greatness, their respiration soars to sixty to seventy breaths per minute. It is a wonderful experiment to periodically, throughout your day, hyperventilate for a few seconds. Feel what it feels like to gush oxygen into every cell, every organ, every action, and every function of your body. What an excellent way to wake your body up and kick yourself into a higher vibrational gear. That is the key. You have the ability to change your internal state at will. Truly, we are self-inspiring human beings. You can choose to be in partnership with the quality of your aging by focusing on generous respirations rather than typical, shallow, adult breaths. Through this practice, you can "re-spirit" yourself at will by pumping oxygen through your body with full, deep belly breaths.

Traditional yogic breathing exercises called pranayama are another way that the body affects the mind and creates the space for inspiration to flow. Modern science now frequently suggests that humans have two brains, one in their heads and one in their nervous system. Both of these brains are derived from the same clump of tissue called the neural crest. During fetal development, one section of the neural crest becomes the central nervous system, and another piece becomes the enteric nervous system located in tissues lining the esophagus, stomach, small intestine, and colon. For this reason, more and more researchers now refer to two brains, one in our head and one in our gut.

It is fitting that this "second brain" is located just below the belly button in the second chakra area. The second chakra is classically known as the point of creativity. Yogis have long known that they can manipulate this second chakra area through physical practices like yoga, meditation, and breathing techniques. These practices stimulate the release of nitric oxide, which in turn floods the body with endorphins and dopamine, thus creating the physical experience of pain, relief, pleasure, and joy. How good it is to know that you are capable of establishing a daily spiritual practice of physical habits that will jump-start positive chemical responses within your body and flood your system with inspiration and creativity.

This ability to affect thoughts, feelings, and creativity via direct manipulation of the body is a concrete, viable tool possessed by all human beings, which puts you in a position of dominion over your availability for inspiration. Imagine that! You have the ability to activate your divine indwelling inspiration through physical actions and focused breathing techniques. Yoga, dance, weight lifting, and running are all excellent entry points for divine inspiration and will be discussed later. The point is that you have a choice. In every moment, in every day, you have the choice to engage in actions and behaviors that open your heart and allow you to breathe in God's grace.

Take a moment and consider what activities awaken your indwelling inspiration. What works for you? Meditation, breathing, dancing, walking, running, biking, hiking, painting, writing, sculpting, gardening, cooking, practicing the presence, what works for you? How can you seed these activities into your daily life? List activities which ignite your inspiration and also note when, throughout your week, you can commit to enjoying them:

1. _____

2. _____

3. _____

4. _____

5. _____

Right here, right now as I breathe in, I open to my highest good. I do not even have to think about it. I breathe and simply say, "Yes." Yes to the biggest vision of my life, the true vision, the true me. Open and receive. Open and illuminate. Open and radiate. This day I choose to move forward being that which I desire. I decide right here and right now to bring it. Whatever good I want to experience in my relationships, I choose to be that good and see it in my beloved as well.

5

Go With the Flow: Your Psychologically Inspired Self

Human psychology involves the mental factors governing a situation or activity. Inspiration has long been associated with specific mental factors which, when activated, spark inspiration within the individual. In Ancient Greece and Rome it was commonly thought that inspiration happened when an artist was transported beyond his own mind while a god's or goddess' mind entered. In this way, the god's mind took over the artist's mind so that the artist could think 'godly' thoughts and produce inspired works. Both Plato and Aristotle agreed that the poet's mind temporarily breaks through to the world of divine truth and this inspired shift in psychology allows inspiration to enter and creation to emerge.

American psychologist Julian Jaynes opined that the phenomenon of inspiration in the form of hearing the voices of muses, spirits, and gods can be explained: He believed that the parieto-temporal location of the right hemisphere of the brain originates auditory signals which are transmitted to the left hemisphere's corresponding Wernicke's area through the anterior commissure—the bundle of nerve fibers that connects the two cerebral hemispheres. In this way, the right, creative mind engages first and then provides direction for the left hemisphere to manifest the inspiration into organized, usable forms. This explains why poetry was originally sung and not written. It also illustrates why music, speeches, and sermons are powerful sources of inspiration because they are activating in a way that makes you more pliable to receive your creativity.

It is interesting to note that in Ancient Greece and Rome, inspiration frequently revealed herself in the form of the divine feminine. Dante led by Beatrice, Socrates guided by Diotima, Athena at the helm of Odysseus' journey, and Faust rescued by Marguerite. This receptive feminine view of inspiration disappeared as psychology, modeled on science, eliminated the feminine as a creative impulse and turned instead to masculine creation, which entails intellect and force. Later, at the dawn of the Renaissance, artists began to own their creations rather than naming the work's source as an outlying mystical temptress.

In modern psychology, inspiration is not frequently studied, but it is generally seen as an internal process. Sigmund Freud located inspiration in the inner psyche, while Carl Gustav Jung's theory of inspiration suggests that it occurs when one is attuned to racial memory, which encodes archetypes of the human mind. Jung saw inspiration as an interruption of the collective unconscious. He wrote that inspiration comes with such force that the conscious, ego self simply gets swept up in the current and the artist merely becomes a helpless observer of events. The inspired work becomes the artist's fate. It is not the artist creating a masterpiece; it is the masterpiece creating an artist.

Throughout the ages, inspiration has been associated with human psychology and mental processes. Former president of the American Psychological Association, Martin Seligman, referred to Mihaly Csikszentmihalyi as the world's leading researcher on positive psychology. This Croatian-born American psychology professor focused his work on the study of happiness, creativity, subjective well-being, and fun. He is best known, however, for his theory on flow, a state of concentration or complete absorption with the activity at hand and the situation.

In *Optimal Experience: Psychological Studies of Flow in Consciousness,* Csikszentmihalyi states that people are most happy when they are in a state of flow, similar to being "in the zone" or "in the groove." The key characteristics of flow are absorption and immersion. This state usually carries with it a sense of great freedom, pleasure, fulfillment, and skill. Another key component of this state is that while one experiences this level of immersion, temporal concerns become insignificant.

Csikszentmihalyi described flow as a state of being completely involved in something for its own sake. Not ego driven or concerned with time; in fact the whole notion of time seems to disappear as one is driven from one absorbed action to the next and the next. Every aspect of yourself is fully engaged. This description of flow is almost identical to Swami Rama Tirtha's description of inspiration. In the moment of true inspiration, there is a full level of absorption. Petty concerns pass by without notice or care. In this zone state of openness, the only thing that matters is diving deeper and deeper into the current. How fully can you let yourself be swept away? How deeply can you immerse yourself?

This reminds me of my New York City days and a tiny little loft apartment I called my tree house. At night, I would climb up a tall wooden ladder into the cave-like loft I slept in. In that sacred space, I often saw angels and spirits. At first, when I saw one benevolent, goddess-like figure, I bolted out of bed in fear. Each night she would show herself, and as soon as I realized what I was seeing, fear drop kicked me out of the experience. With guidance from a shaman, I learned to stay calm in her presence. I learned to talk myself through the experiences by reminding myself that I wanted the connection. I began to welcome her. As I did this, she started staying for longer and longer visits.

One day, while I was visiting with the Native American shaman, she abruptly changed the topic of our conversation and began to complain of a pounding headache. My immediate impulse was to place my hands on the painful area and run energy, but I felt silly offering up my services because she was the professional healer, not me. The more I delayed, the more the shaman reeled in pain. Finally, sheepishly, I asked if I could place my hands on her neck and shoulders. She nodded her head barely looking at me, though in retrospect I do think I saw a twinkle in her eye. Only later did I realize that the twinkle was her way of saying, 'Of course, dumb-dumb, that's the whole point of this charade!'

What's Your What?

As soon as I laid my hands on her, my breath deepened and I felt myself drop into a familiar fathomless void. This was the state I felt at night when I would meet the spirit presence in my tree house loft. It felt like I was gone for hours, though in real time it was about ten minutes. Finally, I drew my hands away and quietly sat in front of the shaman who let me know that her head was restored and expressed her gratitude. We sat for a moment. I felt heavy and far away. She gazed at me patiently and then finally offered, "Perhaps you should go wash your hands." I went into the bathroom and got the shock of a lifetime.

Staring back at me in the reflection of the mirror was the goddess-like presence that visited me at night. My face had become hers and it did not disappear as soon as I saw it. For several minutes, I starred at myself in the mirror. My features had become thicker and more pronounced, clearly Native American. My eyes were larger and a deep chocolate color. I had never experienced anything like it before. When I finally pulled myself away from the mirror, I found my shaman friend standing in the doorway. She was giggling and had a great, big smile on her face. Her work was done. She had taught me how to allow total absorption so well that not only had I learned to be in this angelic presence, I had learned to allow it in so fully that we actually became as one!

The presence of inspiration is similar. It is like welcoming home a mystical, divine goddess. When you get that first burst, that elation, the wash of desire and passion and absolute absorption that is the time to practice talking yourself deeper into the flow state. Consciously note, *Oh, my beloved is here. I choose to be swept away. I allow massive creativity now. I am grateful. I say, 'YES!'* Speaking with yourself in this way is not an intellectual pursuit that would pull you out of the moment, but rather it is a quick acknowledgment and affirmation without stepping out of the event. You let your subconscious mind know that you are grateful and in alignment. This permission opens the floodgates.

Now, here is the kicker, Csikszentmihalyi says that in order to achieve a flow state, a balance must be struck between the challenge of the task and the skill of the performer. If the task is too easy or too difficult, flow cannot occur. So, how does this comply with what we know about inspiration?

Well, I do not find myself overcome with inspiration when I am taking the garbage out or changing my son's poopy diaper, though emersion does sometimes happen with the latter! I do, however, tend to find myself in a zone state of inspiration when I see a sunset, hear a magnificent aria, watch a film that reaches out and grips my heartstrings, hear my child laugh, run barefoot in a forest, dance in a candlelit studio at night, watch crackly, barely visible footage of Reverend Dr. Martin Luther King Jr., or get particularly inciting feedback from someone who matters. Flow happens when it brushes up against your divine purpose, and the same is true of real inspiration. It is tangible and available to you on a regular basis. It is your responsibility, however, to set the stage for an inspired life by consciously training the mental factors governing your daily situations and activities.

What's Your What?

What activities work for you? Recall times in your life when you became so engrossed in something that hours passed like minutes. Recall a time when you no longer cared about getting to the end of a task because the doing was so utterly delicious. List the activities in which you enjoy the highest level of absorption. Create time in your weekly schedule to include these activities. A little goes a long way. If you feel you are already over-tasked, only add one flow state activity into your weekly calendar. Notice what happens. Notice the shifts. Notice openings. You will probably find that other things need to take a back seat so you can get a bit more flow in your week and as more flow enters in the form of absorbing tasks, you will, invariably, notice that your life shifts. It becomes fresh and new. You find more aliveness and your life experiences recalibrate to meet you in your heightened flow state.

Creativity begets creativity. There are times when I feel I am too busy to tend to my drooping blueberry bushes. It feels like I need to stay glued to my desk and work out the next chapter of a book or outline a talk. Yet, once I pull myself away from the blank computer screen, and actually get my hands in the dirt, inspiration gushes forward. Suddenly, I know the direction of the chapter or the content of the talk. That is the beauty of planting absorbing activities in your daily life. They become your launching pad. What flow-inducing activities do you enjoy? Where can you build them into your weekly schedule? Take a moment and list a few choice flow activities and, when you can, incorporate them each week:

1. _____

2. _____

3. _____

4. _____

5. _____

Seed these intentions. Breathe in fully and deeply. Relax. Exhale slowly. Breathe in again. Let the air fill up all the way down into the bottom of your belly. Exhale out slowly and easily. Now imagine breathing in your intention to activate your life by infusing it regularly with these flow-inducing practices. Imagine you are sitting in a fabulous private screening room. Rest easy in a plush reclining chair that wonderfully supports your head, back, and legs. Imagine a large flat screen television in front of you and press play on your remote control.

Begin to view yourself moving through the next week as you most completely desire yourself to be. Envision yourself attending to the details of your life with ease and grace. Notice how good it is to fill your body with foods that are filled with life and energy. Drink in lots of fresh, pure, clear, clean water. Now layer in ample time for your flow-inducing activities, precious moments to write, sculpt, dance, sing, play music, run, meditate, practice yoga, pray, garden, hike, workout, invent, create, craft, or simply play. Let yourself feel how good it feels to get lost in the doing. Feel how good it feels to be in flow, fully absorbed. Notice how you move through your week when you are juiced with intermittent moments of absorption. Notice how you look, how you walk, how you dress, how you care for yourself. Notice a new radiance to your skin tone and sparkle in your eyes. Become aware of all the genius ideas that come to you during your absorbed activity state. How do your interactions with others shift when you are living on point with your purpose by regularly self-inspiring?

Now, rewind the whole film. Press play once again and watch yourself move through the entire week as you most fully desire yourself to be, making sure there are ample moments to indulge in flow. This time as you watch, however, be inside the film. Instead of watching yourself on film, this time be inside of your own movie. See what you see, feel what you feel, hear what you hear, as you live through a week of your life handling the necessary details and sourcing yourself with lush, rich moments lost in elevated states of consciousness as you participate in your flow activities. See what you see, feel what you feel before, during, and after these moments of absorption. Breathe it all in. Breathe in the aliveness. Breathe in the possibility.

One last time, rewind the film and watch it all the way through, viewing yourself so that you are no longer inside of the film, you are back in your comfy screening room reclining chair watching yourself live a week in your life as you most completely desire yourself to be. Be sure your week has a strong balance of flow-inducing activities. Take your time. Breathe and relax. Once you have viewed the film, imagine taking snapshots from the film of your fully engaged, alive self. Plant those snapshots someplace perfect inside of your body. Imagine placing them in your mind, heart, or solar plexus; or you can stamp them into your DNA or sprinkle them all throughout your body like fairy dust!

Breathe in once again, wiggling fingers and toes. Take a luxurious cat stretch. You have done well. You have taken the helm of your consciousness. In this way, you are creating an experiential template for your subconscious mind. You have a new road map. This one includes regular self-restoration, rejuvenation, and "youthening." Let this map guide you through your next week. Let it gush through your experiences with inspiration and vitality. Let it propel you forward and then, return to your comfy imaginary recliner and enjoy the fruits that are, even now, coming to bear...

6

Tickling the Spirit: Setting the Stage for Inspiration

We have been on a hunt, tracking down inspiration, seeking out all of the ways in which it indwells your life naturally. How good it is to know that inspiration is operationally functioning within your physiological, biological, and psychological self. Inspiration works within you, in every moment it is as close as your breath. Inspiration is a cellularly indwelling impulse in the form of syntropy, and a natural aspect of your psyche in the form of inspired flow states. Knowing that you do not have to sit on a mountaintop and wait for the lightning rod of inspiration to strike puts you in the driver's seat of your own destiny. You do not have to wait for those fleeting moments of inspiration to catch you unawares. You are the thing itself. This is the gift God grants to all upon entering life. Each person is given a unique facet of inspiration, a particular way to light the heavens that our universe may spin onwards toward infinity.

Given this good news, we are now back to the beginning question. If inspiration is part of how your mental, spiritual, and physical self works, how do you let it work for you? How can you learn to court and nurture this wispy treasure so that you may live more and more in that highest of highs, Divine Inspiration? More than that, how can you let your spark of inspiration carry you through to the finish line so that your radiant life purpose may be fully realized in your lifetime?

We all come in on a dream. It is as though you were on a conveyor belt up in Heaven and just before you were about to drop down into human form, the seed of something special was placed inside of you. It is your "what," that thing for which you were born. Some people may think that conveyor belt must have malfunctioned the day they were born. "So-and-so definitely got two seeds of special-ness, and the one I got was defunct!" Not so. We all come in on a dream and the dream is an achievable one. It would not come into your consciousness as a soul desire if it was not for you. So, the question is, what's your what, and how are you doing with it?

The big news flash here—it is on you to muse yourself. It is your responsibility to do whatever it takes to keep yourself fresh and available for the full revelation of your purpose. I heard a story once, a simple story, about a guy who went out for a run. Mundane as it gets. But this particular guy chose to run in a place that full tilt stoked his inspiration.

He began telling his story by saying that he likes to run along the Mall. When I first heard that, I got excited. I thought, *Perfect. He likes the mall, I like the mall. We are kindred spirits, great!* Then

What's Your What?

I realized he was speaking of the Mall in Washington, D.C., home of many of America's great national monuments. Some people get excited about places of massive social and historical significance, and others get excited at places that sell inappropriately high-heeled shoes. What can I say?!

At any rate, something happened inside of me as I heard this guy's story. He spoke of the different monuments and memorials that he passed along his run each day. He spoke of gazing up at the Lincoln Memorial at night when no one was around, reading the Gettysburg Address and the Second Inaugural Address, looking out over the Reflecting Pool, and imagining the vast crowd captivated by Dr. King's impassioned dream. As I heard the telling of this story, I could almost feel the caldron of creation beginning to brew, the primordial soup of his soul waking up, simmering with inspiration. This is what we can do. This is what you must do. We must be self-inspiring. Why? Because you live in a culture that is structured on mediocrity, plagued with epidemic normalcy, the contagion of complacency at every turn. At every corner, opportunities to numb out and dim down, drive thru, fast food, dead food restaurants, and endless hours of television watching.

According to the A.C. Nielsen Co., the average American watches television approximately two months per year. Two months worth of time every year spent watching TV! The amount of television watched increases as a person ages so by the time the average person is sixty-five years old they will have spent approximately nine years of life, glued to the tube. We absolutely must choose to be self-inspiring. You must seat yourself smack in the middle of that divine ache that Martha Graham spoke of to Agnes de Mille. She was referring to artists, but we are all artists crafting the masterpiece of our lives. Graham said that we live with a divine dissatisfaction. It is a need that lives within you. This need is the seed of specialness placed inside your soul at birth. It is your soul intent, that urge that is ever beckoning you forward. When you answer this need, when you walk in its direction, it floods you with magical aliveness.

You have felt this. Those moments kissed by inspiration, the ones that light you up with possibility and catapult you forward with energy and focus. We must live lives that seat us smack in the center of our own divine dissatisfaction, that straddle point of standing one foot inside of your dream and always one foot outstretched, leaping forward toward fuller expression.

The truth is that you know who you are. You know what you are meant for. You have felt it, gotten tastes of it. Not only do you know who you are, usually, you know early on. Life regularly creates opportunities and experiences for self-revelation and these opportunities begin even in our earliest years. When I was about thirteen years old, my city's public school council decided to eliminate the arts program. I had a problem with that, so I wrote a letter to the editor of our big city newspaper. I will always remember the day that paper came thumping up against our front door, unrolling it, peeling back the pages, and then seeing my name and my thoughts and convictions in print. It was like the whole world had a chiropractic adjustment and everything in life felt well-aligned. A short time later, I was invited to speak at a large city hearing to discuss the removal of arts in education. There was a huge crowd, all of the education officials, government officials, a bank of media cameras and microphones, and then there was me, as shy and introverted as they come. Yet I got up in front of everyone, no holds barred, and spoke my convictions. The world made sense. I felt right in my own skin. When was the last time you felt right in your skin, felt like you were being exactly who you are meant to be?

Take a moment and recall a time in your life when you felt unstoppable. Full throttle. When you felt at home in your own skin and even if the task at hand challenged you, in fact it probably did, you felt yourself thrive within the challenge. Rise into your divinity. Recall a time in your life when you were, even for a moment, doing what you were meant to do. If you cannot recall an actual time, then make one up. Your subconscious mind cannot discern the difference between a real or imagined event so juice your system with the "remembered" experience of being completely who you are meant to be. Describe it fully. What did it feel like to express yourself in this way? How did you feel in your body? What are the predominant qualities that you experienced?

_____

_____

_____

Can you imagine if we stopped right there? If you took what you knew about yourself and the seed of something special placed within you and devoted the next days, weeks, months, years of your life to grooming and growing those qualities within you? Unfortunately, too many people spend years, sometimes a lifetime, searching all around the glaringly obvious for something that fits in better, makes more sense, is less controversial, or easier to explain to Mom and Dad.

You know who you are. You know the dream that lives inside of you and the deal is, it is doable. It would not come to you as a soul desire if it were not for you. Here is a clue, it is not a purple convertible Bentley. What you are born for has no top. It is not completable in your lifetime. You are here to shine as the many faces of God: peace, love, joy, harmony, balance, ease, truth, justice, integrity, honor, courage, wisdom, prosperity, and abundance. However, while each of us possesses all of these qualities, there are usually particular ones that have extra juice for you. Even though you know what your what is, deep down inside that "what" can sometimes feel miles away, covered up with the dirt and grit from life's journey. That is when you need to go on an archeological dig to self-resuscitate. If you want more clarity about why you are here, there are simple ways to gain clarity and confirm the guidance that you are already getting from your daily spiritual practice of prayer, meditation, and Life Visioning.

What's Your What?

The first exercise to obtain clarity is to pull out all of the old year-books, cards, letters, and emails that you have received over the years. Make a list of every adjective that has ever been used to describe you. Every *positive* adjective that has been used to describe you! You can even send out a mass email or Facebook request asking all of your contacts to send you their top three positive adjectives for you. Next, tally up the results of how many times each of the main adjectives were used. Notice themes, similar words or synonyms and lump them together. You will realize that you have always been seen. The essence of you, the qualities that you are here to shine as, are undeniable. You have even been seen by the people you say never understood you or do not know who you really are. There may be people in your life that do not agree with your choices or understand your way of going about things; however, you will find that even the ones you think, "Don't get me," have seen who you truly are. It is fascinating to realize that you have already been giving the gift you were God-given to give!

A second exercise you can do to gain clarity regarding your life purpose is quite revealing though a bit more time consuming. It involves hanging out around large groups of bored people. Take a sheet of paper and list a few hundred adjectives on it. Get a buddy and go find a crowd with nothing to do. I did this when you could still walk through airports and ask people who were waiting for delayed planes to participate, but a movie theater line or any other place with lots of people who have some time will also do well. Have your friend hand out a copy of the adjective paper to several people while you stand a few yards away, but still in the sight line of the crowd. You say nothing and do nothing. The people are asked to check off all the adjectives that they feel apply to you. These are people you do not know and with whom you have had no interaction. Yet when you tally up the results and focus on the top five most checked off adjectives, you will be amazed to see how transparent the truth of you really is. You are seen, without even trying! The essence of who you really are is undeniable.

This feedback process is designed to help you fine tune the nature of your life's purpose, the specific way in which you are inspiration. For example, if one of the top adjectives that comes up for you is fun, then the passion that you follow had best include fun. If one of the top adjectives is wisdom, then acting airy or dumb will keep you out of alignment. Once you claim yourself as Wisdom and *own it*, it is like a puzzle fitting into the right slot. You plug in and the light that you emit is true and unique. Your full, clear brand of inspiration is a vital ingredient in the overall well being of our planet. It may sound silly to go through so much work to discover who you are, but we human beings are filled with complexities. Oftentimes people have layered facade after facade, coping mechanism after coping mechanism, until the face they show the world is a distorted version of the truth and they do not even know it. This process is one of recalling the real you, your real nature, and raising it up in its multifaceted brilliance.

Another way to clarify your "what" is to recall the kinds of things you used to love to do when you were younger. I once had a client in my office who was bored and unclear. She did not know what to do with herself; life had not worked out the way she had hoped. I asked her what she used to love to do as a child. She dispassionately rattled off a few things: dolls, drawing, etcetera. Then all of a sudden I saw a glint in her eye. The color in her cheeks began to flush and her respiration increased. "Basketball. I loved playing basketball," she said. "Great," I said, but before I could get another word out, she cut me off. "I know what you are going to say. You are going to suggest that I join some old ladies' basketball league. No thank you!" Actually, I was *not* going to suggest that she join an "old ladies'" basketball league, but I did ask her if there was any other way she could be involved with basketball, since it had once given her so much joy.

She quickly dismissed the thought, and then slowly, shyly, she mentioned that it had occurred to her to maybe coach the girls' basketball team at the local YWCA. You see! We know! She already had the feeling, the impulse to do it, but sometimes it takes a while to believe what we know. She started coaching the girls' basketball team and now she is back in business. Her life has juice and that enthusiasm spills over into every other area of her life, her relationships, the way she cares for herself, her prosperity, on and on. It is like, "Houston, we have lift off!" She is back in the game. All we need to do is get back to the what. What do you love, what lights you up? Then, let God figure out the how and gently whisper clues into your subconscious mind.

Growing up, running was my thing. My knees are not interested in running now and I would not want to be a coach, so I asked myself, what was the quality I felt when I was running? What made it so compelling? It was easy for me to determine the quality I felt when I ran: freedom...absolute, soaring, off the charts, can do and be anything, freedom.

When you find the quality that sends you, that soars you, that flies you, you will follow it anywhere, and with good reason. That quality is the key to unlocking your indwelling wellspring of inspiration. For example, I met a really cute guy one time and he asked me out on a date. He invited me out on a completely typical date, the kind of date any girl would love. He invited me to a party on a Saturday night. But this guy did not know who I really was or that I was not available for his Saturday night party because I already had the hottest plans in town—crazy, awesome, thrilling plans.

My plans were so amazing that I knew I could not be selfish; I had to invite this cute guy to join me. So, I explained to him that I could not go to a party with him because I was choosing to spend my Saturday driving a few hours in the middle of the night to a cemetery to watch authentic footage of Reverend Dr. Martin Luther King Jr. Why? Because freedom is my thing. Freedom is the quality that energizes me most and Dr. King is the brand of freedom that sends me and soars me and fills me with the same kind of all-things-possible energy that I felt when I would run hard and fast, round and round my block at night as a teenager. If it has to do with Dr. King, I am there.

Have you ever been on a date with someone and seen that glaze come over their eyes that lets you know it is just not going to happen? As I told the cute guy about my big Saturday night plans, I saw the glaze settle over his eyes as he slowly backed away declining the invitation to join me at the cemetery on Saturday night. But that is just fine because whoever you end up with has to respect the ache, that longing that lives inside of you. If they do not respect your ache, it just has to be, "bye bye." No questions asked, just, "bye bye."

I was once set up on a blind date. Before I even met the man, I told all of my girlfriends I was going to marry him because on paper he was everything I had ever wanted. Finally, he flew into town to meet me. This was hardcore; he literally took a plane ride to meet me! I just knew it was going to be the perfect romantic story that we would tell the rest of our happily married lives.

Honestly, I was not attracted to him, at all. That did not matter, though. I was still going to marry him because on paper he was everything I had ever wanted. We went out to dinner and shared our hopes and dreams. I got up the courage to share with him my crazy pipe dream that one day I would serve with Michael Bernard Beckwith as a trans-denominational (inclusive of all religions) minister at Agape International Spiritual Center. Everything was going great. At the end of the date, he told me how wonderful I am, what an awesome time he had, and he let me know, however, that he could never be with a minister. That would not work for him. There is only one answer at that point: "bye bye." That is when you need to dropkick them to the curb. Whoever you choose has to respect your ache. It is your what. You cannot be a *who* without a *what*, so do not give that away to anyone for anything!

Back to cute guy and my hot Saturday night plans. Finally, the night of my big plans rolled around. I jumped into my Jeep and took off. I was driving on freeways I had never been on before, completely alone. At last, I pulled into a huge cemetery, pitch black. I was scared and completely out of my element, but following my ache. I knew I had to be there; I had to be where freedom is. I finally got where I needed to go, found a seat, and dove in. I was utterly riveted watching authentic footage of Reverend Dr. Martin Luther King Jr. When you source yourself in this way, it is like being hooked up on life support. There I was, getting my fix.

About an hour in, I felt a tap on my shoulder. Cute guy! The cute guy, who had invited me to the party, showed up at the cemetery instead! I offered him the seat next to me and we sat quietly watching the film for a few minutes. Then he tapped me on the shoulder and politely asked, "Can you understand anything they're saying?" It was authentic 1960s footage, all crackly and inaudible. "No," I said. "I can't understand a thing. Shush!" And I went back to watching because I did not care that I could not understand anything being said. For me, it was the thrill of having any kind of proximity to someone who so fully represents what most enlivens me.

Another few minutes passed. Cute guy tapped me on the shoulder again, "Can you make out any of the images on the screen?" The film was so old, black and white, filled with static and barely visible. "No," I said and went right back to watching because in my mind, who cares if I cannot see it or hear it. I am just happy to soak up whatever I can get. A long stretch of time passed and finally cute guy said to me, "Are you good?" I took a deep, full breath. "Yes. I am good," I said. I had gotten my fix. I had juiced my life purpose, and yes, I was deeply content. We got up, walked out of the cemetery, and you can be damn sure I married *that* man!

They have to respect the ache. Whatever your ache is, whoever you choose to be in a relationship with, they must respect the ache. They do not have to have the same ache as you. They do not have to do your ache with you, but they must respect your ache.

First and foremost, you must respect your own ache. When you give over fully to that thing for which you were born, when you acknowledge it and commit to it, you will find that you attract people into your life who respect your need for self-realization. You will also notice that as you fully commit to outwardly be who you inwardly are, your full brilliance, the people in your life, whether they agree with what you are doing or how you are doing it, usually get on board. Some may fall away, even if only temporarily, but the riches of saying, "Yes!" to your soul's longing will, in the end, outweigh any attempt to sacrifice yourself in order to keep someone else around.

I once asked my husband why he drove out to the cemetery that night. He told me that when he was in college, his friend's dad gave him girl advice. Referring to girls, the father said, "They're all crazy. You just have to find your kind of crazy." My husband said that he realized I was his kind of crazy! My prayer for you is that you find your kind of crazy and that you continue to follow your ache because when you do, everything is possible.

Take a moment to activate the Universal Law of Manifestation. Begin by deciding that your good is at hand. Choose to believe that this is so. Declare that right where you are, your perfect kind of crazy in this moment shines forth in all areas of your life in the form of partners, friends, beloveds, communities, and work space. Let your joyous expectancy attract all manner of good to you this very day! Take in a full, deep breath. Release it all out. Breathe in another full, deep, easy breath. On the exhalation release anything and anyone that no longer serves your soul's high calling. May you be richly blessed and surrounded by those who either share your ache or those who inspire a creatively conducive environment to help you fulfill it.

This is how it works. You do whatever it takes to place yourself in the center of your ache and stay intimately close to that which inspires you, like that guy who went out for a run. As he ran, his soul's clarity of purpose alchemically mixed with the bones of this nation's history. Something began simmering deep down in his soul as he stood right where Dr. King stood. I could almost feel the tidal wave of inspiration cresting as he continued speaking of his run along the Mall in Washington, D.C.

He said it made him think of America and all of the different people who played a role in creating it. He thought of how each person with their unique gifts and skills was so crucial in the overall fabric of America. He spoke of how much had to be overcome, the struggles and challenges and all of the nameless, faceless people whose blood, sweat, and tears built this land now enjoyed by millions. His passion was palpable as was the earnestness of his desire.

Then the full-on tsunami of inspiration crashed down upon him, shattering anything unlike itself, so that the only thing left stood simple and raw as he uttered with an almost childlike prayer, how very much he wants to be a part of the process of building a true United States of America.

How could then Senator Barack Obama not become president in 2009 with a yearning that deep? It was his what. Whether or not you agree with his politics, the point is that he had a soul need that drove him. He did the work of self-inspiring by placing himself in environments that propelled his inspiration. That kind of fueled desire cannot be denied. What is yours? What wants to emerge through you right now? What is your ache? Are you willing?

We move toward self-perfection and fulfillment because it is part of our biologically encoded impulse to do so. We also move toward the realization of our gifts because the neighbor to your left needs you to, because the neighbor to your right requires it. Because the person in front of you on the freeway and the person behind you in the grocery store line, the people in this state and the next, the people in our country and all countries, cannot make it without you. The earth has been here billions of years before you and it will be here billions of years after you, but you and I, we need each other. We have nothing without each other.

You are part of a grand mosaic; every piece counts. Someone is here to save the dolphins, someone is here to save the whales, someone is keeping our oceans clean, and someone is tidying up the beaches. Someone is here to make sure we have a sustainable environment so that seven times seven generations beyond us may enjoy life. Someone is here to make sure our wise ones, our elders, have proper medical care and housing, so that they may enjoy their latter years with dignity and respect. Someone is here to make damn sure that every child's belly is filled and body respected. Where are you? We need you. Your presence is needed. Someone is here to make us laugh because otherwise the ridiculousness of it all would drop us. Someone is here to crack our hearts wide open with the exquisite pain and beauty of their art so that we may stay compassionate and sentient beings.

When you feel tired and do not think you can keep on keeping on, that is the moment to go back to your what. Root yourself in your what because in your what all things are possible. A guy on a run becomes President of the United States of America. A girl in a cemetery meets the man of her dreams. Your life is for you. Your life is for you. Hear that. Say it to yourself, *"My life is for me."*

"My life is for me." Feel it. Imagine it. Imagine if you believed it. Imagine if you allowed it. "My life is for me." The whole world has to recalibrate itself to meet you where you live in this highly convicted understanding. Your life is for you, and it is on you, every moment of every day to show your life that you are for it!

7

Muse Yourself

At this point you should have clear insight into your particular brand of inspiration. The good news is that the clearer you are with what you put out in the world, the clearer the universe's response. This new clarity is vital because as opportunities arise, they either fit into your purpose, which makes them a "yes," or they do not, and it becomes an easy "no." Armed with a clear knowledge of who you are and how you have come into the world to shine, you are like a surfer in the ocean waiting to catch a wave of inspiration. It is now time to learn key ways to coax movement from flat waters.

The million-dollar question is, how does inspiration get triggered? It happened to Einstein while riding a streetcar. Nietzsche got it by glancing down at a block of stone. Tesla was struck with it when out for a stroll, and Archimedes got it while splashing about in a bath.

The 'it' is inspiration. This heightened state is commonly referred to by a plethora of names: enlightenment, illumination, insight, intuition, vision, discovery, or revelation. All of these titles represent the same type of experience, a transportation in consciousness from common thinking into a fully illumined state of mental processes, which manifest as inspired creations. Inspiration brings a heightened state of clarity, a new perspective, or the feeling of glimpsing the world in a new way. Others describe it as a veil being lifted. Questing is one way of describing the journey toward inspiration. Carl Jung's description was a bit more graphic. In *Seven Sermons to the Dead* (1916), Jung called it "the eternally sucking gorge of the void." Whether you strive toward it or are overcome by it, the reaching is the same.

Let us look at how some people are successfully allowing inspiration to illuminate their lives. Michael Bernard Beckwith receives inspiration by using a transformational inner technology called The Life Visioning Process. This is a conscious process of activating one's highest potential through four stages of consciousness. His work is about guiding individuals from the victim consciousness stage, to the manifester stage, and on to the third stage where one surrenders to a higher intelligence. The fourth stage is about *being* consciousness, which manifests as enlightened living.

The actual practices that he uses include: meditation, affirmative prayer, the Life Visioning Process, and insights from numerous diverse traditions. In his book, *The Life Visioning Process* (2008), he says that the culmination of this process allows for an intuitive awareness of "God's idea of itself as your life." Having a clear, direct awareness of God's idea of itself as your life equals Absolute Inspiration. There can be no higher thing to aspire to than the fulfillment of being that for which you were born.

Wayne Dyer discusses how to start an inspiration practice in his book, *Inspiration: Your Ultimate Calling* (2007). He prescribes five daily practices to establish an inspired life. The first is to commit to at least one daily experience where you share yourself and have no expectation of being thanked or acknowledged. The gesture can be big or small; the point is to begin each day in conscious alignment with Spirit. The second practice is about becoming conscious of any thoughts that are not in alignment with your Source. When judgment or a sense of separation comes into your mind, Dyer advises that you stay in spiritual alignment and make a silent effort to shift your thoughts to match Source energy.

Another practice Dyer advises is to take one or two minutes of quiet time with God before sleeping and upon awakening. Be in a state of appreciation and tell yourself that you are choosing to feel good. The power in this practice is that it places you in dominion of your life. It gives you the moment to consciously decide your good. The fourth practice is to remind yourself that your life is bigger than you are. Your life is Spirit flowing through you. This creates the opening and availability for inspiration to enter. It lets you rest in the knowing that you do not have to do everything. There is a higher power present. You only need to know the "what" of your desire, what you want, and let this higher power figure out the how. The final daily practice is to dedicate your life to something that reflects an awareness of your Divinity. This is a silent acknowledgement of your own Divine nature. Whether the people around you get it or not, you know who and "whose" you are and you say, YES!

Many physical activities can be perfect springboards for creativity. While the physical body is kept busy pumping iron in a gym, running along a wooded path, swimming laps, dancing, practicing yoga, painting, sculpting, or any number of activities, the physical, rhythmic engagement can be used to create a light hypnotic state. This relaxes the conscious mind enough that the critical faculty, that aspect of your consciousness that judges, accesses, and criticizes, can become relaxed enough that you gain heightened access to your subconscious mind. This is the opportunity to tap directly into your creative wellspring. These physical activities trigger a surge of increased blood flow to the brain, which impacts brain chemistry and contributes to an altered state of consciousness. How exceptional to know that through physically initiated activities, you can open yourself to the kinds of altered states of consciousness that act as portals into divine inspiration. The ways and means of accessing inspiration are as numerous and varied as are human beings.

Reflect on the various activities you like to participate in and list the ones that you find most absorbing. It is likely that when you engage in these practices, you will often find yourself most creative, bubbling over with inspired ideas. You will be invited to do this process a few times over the course of this book. It is like peeling away layers of an onion. Notice if anything new bubbles up. The more you write this process out, the more it becomes committed into your consciousness. This makes it more likely for you to remember to initiate these activities on a regular basis so that they may become reflexive and habitual. List activities that you find both absorbing and enjoyable:

1. _____

2. _____

3. _____

4. _____

5. _____

We now know that the above practices create an optimum internal environment for inspiration to fountain up. Prayer, gratitude, visualization, Life Visioning Process, yoga, painting, running, dancing, group trances, time in nature, and prayer rituals are all natural practices that coax open the doors of your little self and make entry for inspiration. You are now in the driver's seat. You are no longer at the whim of your inspiration. You have dominion and you may choose right now to prime yourself with daily practices so that this very night you may sup with the Divine.

This day I open in availability and consciousness, allowing Divine Source, which is everywhere, to light me up like a lightning bolt with all manner of inspired thoughts, words, and deeds.

8

What Happened on the 8th Day? Moving from Self-activated Inspiration to Surrendered Swoon

What happened on the eighth day? This is a good question, right? After all, we know what happened on days one through seven. On the first day, God created day and night and said it was good. On the second day, God created the sea and sky and said it was good. On the third day, God created earth and her fruits and on the fourth day God did a little decorating and hung up some lights—the sun, moon, and stars. On the fifth day, God created the creatures of the air and ocean, and on the sixth day God created land animals and man. From man, we all know, God drew forth a single rib, and from that *one* rib God created mood swings, chocolate cravings, and the uncanny ability to speak for really, really long periods of time about feelings—Woman! And God said she was good!

As the sun rose on the morning of the seventh day, God declared it a day of rest, a holy, sacred day, the Sabbath. God blended a green drink and spent the whole day flipping back and forth between *Game of Thrones* and *The Real Housewives of the Garden of Eden*. This much we know. We know about the creation story, but what happened on the eighth day? That is the day we began expanding in consciousness and deepening in devotion. Here is how it went down:

On the morning of the eighth day, God looked out at all that had been created and God said, to you, *I have given you everything. I have given you the best of me. I have given you all of me. I went to town on this whole building a universe thing. I gave you mountains and oceans, deserts and valleys. I gave you, my sons and my daughters, consciousness and creativity. I have given it all to you. At this point, it is on you.*

However, God said, *there are two criteria I need you to know. First, since we are all one, all connected—by me—*God said, *what I am going to do is individualize this whole living a life deal. Each of you came into life with certain key areas to grow into and as you do so, you do your part in evolving the whole of humanity forward. For example, some people will be growing in the area of prosperity and money. Some will be working it out in the area of health and wholeness. Others will be stretching in love, relationships, family, and connection. Some will have horrible childhoods and will spend their time moving beyond that. Others will have wonderful childhoods and still grow up to be great big hot messes. Everyone will have something, and in your overcoming you will do your part in evolving humankind.*

What's Your What?

That is the first piece, God said. *There will be challenges along your way. The second thing I need you to know is that you are never alone. I will always be with you. I will walk this walk with you every step of the way. When you are running, I will run with you and soar with you when you are flying. Whether you are on your hands and knees or if the most you can muster is a belly crawl, I will be with you, always. To ease your journey, I will provide light posts along your way, moments of inspiration to keep you keeping on.*

I will bring in a young girl with her leg all gnarled and twisted. Doctors will say she will never walk right and will be stuck in a leg brace her whole life. Yet she will literally run that brace right off of her leg and into Olympic gold medal history as the fastest woman in the universe. I am going to show you that there is always possibility. We will let a good man sit in a bad jail for twenty-seven years and emerge with a smile that could still light the heavens, radiant and joy-filled. He will go on to become president of the country that held him prisoner and he will set up forgiveness tribunals where there were war tribunals. I am telling you, the Lord said, *No matter what challenges you may have on your plate from time to time, I will show you that there is always a way.*

We will send some folks up to the moon and have them walk around up there just because we can. We will have a woman become mother to the poorest of the poor, the sickest of the sick, and she will drop us to our collective knees with the humbling teaching that if you have no peace, it is because you have forgotten that we belong to each other. We belong to each other. Is that not extraordinary? What a comfort. How lovely to know that you are not meant to do it all yourself. In fact, you can't. It is on us to take care of each other. It is on us to support one another. Support our communities. Support humanity, yes?

I will bring in a young teenager and have her write a wartime diary, God said. *Even while those who share her religious beliefs are being murdered by the millions, she will have it within herself to say that despite everything, she still believed that people are really good at heart.* That is who you are. You have been born with your own internal re-fresh button. You can begin again at any moment. You are renewable. You can be fresh and new, buoyant and energized, no matter what you have done or where you have been. There is a core essential essence of you that cannot be hurt, harmed, or tarnished no matter what. *I will show you and show you and show you,* the Lord said, *until my showing becomes your knowing.*

That is what happened on the eighth day. God told us there would be challenges along our way, but also let us know that we would be given inspirational sustenance. *Not only will I give you inspiration,* God said, *but you are a source of inspiration. I have made you in my image and likeness and goodness and therefore you are meant to be a source of inspiration as well.* When was the last time you were a source of inspiration for yourself or someone else? Think of a time when you said or did something that made someone else's day. Perhaps you showed up at just the right time and your presence was the difference that made the difference.

It does not have to be a great, big heroic feat. Sometimes it can be the most simple of gestures. It can be a wave, a hug, or perhaps just letting someone get in front of you on the freeway. We never know what is going on inside another person's life and sometimes the most basic act of human civility can be just enough to talk someone down off a ledge that you did not even know they were teetering on. Or it could be the moment that sets someone soaring when all they needed was a little loving nudge, a moment of support that lets them know, "I've got your back. There is support. There is connection. All is well. We're with you." It is the simple gestures that often make the biggest impact.

I recently went to Texas to visit my grandfather. When I entered his room, I found a dramatic scene unfolding. My grandfather was crying and telling the nurses that he loved them. The nurses where crying and telling my grandpa that they loved him. My grandfather was saying good-bye to everyone and letting them know that he was, in fact, dying. I adore my grandpa, so understandably this was a lot to take in. I took a deep breath and quietly walked over to his bedside. I sat next to him, closed my eyes, and breathed.

I breathed for the first hour while nurses and medical attendants rushed around my anxious grandfather. I breathed for the second hour and the room became a bit more calm. A few people left and my grandfather began to settle a bit. I breathed for the third hour and finally it was just my grandpa and me, and he began to doze off peacefully. I breathed for the fourth hour, and during that fourth hour my grandpa awoke. He took my hand in both of his hands—those hands of his that I had been holding my whole life. For my whole life, his hands seemed to be the biggest hands in the world. He took my hand in his hands that now felt to me so delicate and fragile, like little bird bones loosely draped in skin. He pulled me in close so we were face to face, and he whispered, "You have no idea what you have just done. You have given me fresh life."

That is all it takes, a moment of kindness. A moment of your presence can be life support for another. That is what happened on the eighth day. God told us there would be challenges along our way; that is part of the deal. God let us know that inspiration would be provided to keep us moving forward, and that we, in fact, carry a moral mandate to be a source of inspiration as well. With this clarity, God whispered gently to us once again, *I have given you everything. At this point, it is on you. Do what you can do.*

We humans first began by expanding our consciousness and learning how to use what we have been given. Adam was out cruising around the Garden of Eden one day when he had the genuine thought: *I wish I could get a front row parking space right in front of the Tree of Knowledge. I just wish I could get right up front. I am so tired of having to park and walk!* He turned the corner and, BAM! Front row parking space right in front of the Tree of Knowledge! *What a wonderful coincidence,* he thought. Next day Adam was out and about doing his thing when all of a sudden he had a strong longing feeling, *Oh, I wish Eve would call. I really wish she would call. I am still angry about that whole apple incident, but I sure would love to hear from her.* BAM! Text message from Eve! Now Adam knew that he was on to something. He grabbed Eve and said, *I figured out how we work. If you have a thought and fill it with intense emotion, it happens!* Well this was thrilling news for Eve because she wanted to lose those last five pounds but nothing was working. Now she knew what to do. She thanked Adam and went on her way confident that she would soon lose the weight.

A few days passed and nothing happened. Eve did not lose weight. She became depressed. We all know what happens to Eve when she becomes depressed—she eats! There Eve was, devouring a coconut bowl full of Haagen Dazs ice cream, when Adam came wandering around the corner. He took one look at her and already, by day eight, Adam instinctively knew he should put himself into reverse and get the heck out of there! But it was too late. Eve had seen him, and so, already by day eight, Adam knew what he needed to do. He walked over and sat on the tree stump opposite Eve and said, *If you are having any feelings that you would like to share, I am available to listen.* (He was a very well-trained Adam!)

Between mouthfuls of ice cream, Eve immediately began unloading her feelings; *It's just not fair. I am doing everything you said, and I'm still not losing the weight. I have a clear thought because I definitely want to lose the weight, and my thought is definitely backed by tremendous emotion because I cannot stand this muffin-top action rolling over the top of my fig leaf, but it is still not working! I'm so frustrated...* At this point Adam realized that he had gotten himself into a bind. He had the answer. He knew why Eve's attempts to lose weight were failing, but he also knew—already, by day eight—that he was supposed to be listening and not fixing, so he held his tongue as Eve continued expressing her disappointment.

Finally, Adam could not hold it in any longer. He burst out, *I am so sorry, I know that I am supposed to be listening and not fixing, but I have the answer! Yes, in order to create something you need to have a clear thought fueled by intense emotion, but I messed up. I forgot the next step. You have to DO something. It would not have done me any good if I had just lain around the house thinking, "I wish I had a front row parking space in front of the Tree of Knowledge." No! I had to get in my Tesla. I had to drive over to the tree to get my parking space and claim my good! Oh,* said Eve, *I get it now.* Eve immediately began taking action. She started doing Zumba in the garden and practicing portion control. Before she knew it, she was lean and mean, comfortably fitting into her fig leaf again. That is what happened on the eighth day. We learned to use what we have to be who we want.

We also learned how to use our consciousness to release what no longer serves. I realized at one point that I had a habit of walking around with my head down. This is not a particularly big deal. In fact, I tend to wear inappropriately high-heeled shoes so walking with my head down probably prevents me from tripping all over myself. However, it became clear to me that the feeling of walking with my head down is very different than the feeling of walking around with my head held high, and I realized that my physiology had created a very subtle, yet insidious, way of having me basically walk around apologizing for my life. Hiding out. Laying low. Ducking from the next blow. Flying under the radar. Anybody relate?

There are many similar habits or behaviors that on their own are not such a big deal, yet they have a cumulative way of crimping energy or blocking flow, and I do not want anything impeding the flow of your genius. Some of the subtle behaviors that can do that are things like hunched shoulders, lack of eye contact, taking little sips of air into the chest rather than full, deep belly gulps of life, and speaking in a voice that is not within your authentic vocal range. This is especially common with women who are often taught that a higher voice is cute.

I take a yoga class that is incredibly challenging. The teacher is like an Amazon. She stalks us back and forth across the yoga studio pushing all of the students further than they think they can go. She is strong and powerful and utterly in dominion for the entire class, until the last sixty seconds when it is her time to sell herself, to share her products, workshops, and upcoming events. During those last sixty seconds, all of a sudden her voice gets very high and girlishly wishy-washy. It is a stunning transformation. I literally show up week after grueling week and wreck myself in this intense class for the sheer psychological profile study of watching a grown, competent woman release all of her power when it is time to ask for what she wants in life. This is what I call the subtle insidious. Small behaviors that leak, drain, block, or negate energy.

Why do these behaviors appear? The blunt answer is that it does not matter. What matters is that you do whatever it takes to become more and more available to your indwelling inspiration. However, sometimes a little conscious content is useful, so it is okay to get a bit of understanding about why things are the way they are. Habitual defending behaviors often establish themselves early on in life after someone has said or done something to which you immediately receive an unconscious message that protection is necessary. The defenses can also go up after you have said or done something and based upon the response you received, a clear unconscious decision gets made: *Wow, that person really did not like how bright I am. I better dim down my wattage.* A simple look or an unkind word from someone who matters can be enough to derail a life. It is our responsibility to get back on track, and we can!

While these energy crimping behaviors can become established during the course of one's life, they can also be passed down through a person's lineage. We humans have been around for about two hundred and fifty thousand years. It makes sense that some consciousness sediment would accumulate along the way, debris of thoughts and beliefs from generations past. We belong to many tribes, many peoples who lived long before us. You have your family tribe, the line of your blood relations. You have the tribe of people who have the same color skin you have, the same religion, the same politics, gender, sexual orientation, and preference. All of these peoples have clearly defined, usually unspoken, unconscious rules about who and what you can be, do, and have based it upon their experiences.

You want to make sure that you are available to the excellence and possibility of the present moment, not mired by the past. How do you dust off old, unhelpful belief systems? Rebirthing is one useful tool. It is the purposeful practice of rapid breathing with a trained specialist to help slough off old emotions. Conscious breath work can be a great way to ventilate and stay fresh. You can also simply focus on slow, full, deep belly breaths while affirming that which you do desire. For example, breathe in deeply while slowly counting to four. Hold for a count of eight, and release for a count of four. When I do this I create affirmations with the number of syllables that I am counting during each step and then, rather than count, I internally recite the affirmation. For example:

I (1) am (2) free (3) now. (4)
I (1) let (2) God's (3) vision (4,5) guide (6) my (7) way. (8)
Grateful (1,2) Thankful. (3,4)

Simply taking five minutes to breathe with positive intention can be enough to bring you fully into this present moment. You can also practice setting an intention before you work out. Physical activity coupled with intention and passionate music is exceptionally powerful because it blends the movements of your body with the positive intentions and emotion that you want. Your cells become infused with present-moment conscious choices. Other wonderful ways to get out of the past and allow the total flow of your energy now, are regularly practicing prayer, meditation, and visioning. I want God's vision running my life, not the subjective vision of those who came before me. I can honor and appreciate where I come from, my many tribes, but I choose God as the captain of my ship, don't you?

When you do the regular maintenance work to keep yourself and your thoughts clean and clear, you find yourself flooded with new-found energy. It is your job to constantly elevate the baseline of your consciousness. As you do so, you are now able to thrive as a force of impact and effectiveness.

I had a client once who had an interesting situation. Each month at the time of her menstruation, she went to the hospital because of extreme pain. By the time she arrived at my office, she was on daily anti-depressants and anti-anxiety medication. I guided her into a hypnotic state and then began using various techniques with her to gain clarity about the situation. About an hour into the process, she became very still. Her eyes popped wide open and she said to me, "I'm done." My ego kicked in and the first thing I thought was, *I am the facilitator of this session. I get to say when we are done, not her!* Fortunately, I kept my mouth shut. It is a good thing that I did because her floodgates had just opened wide and there was much that was now ready for full release. She *was* done; done with holding in decades of long buried pain that had finally made its way to the surface.

As a teenager, she had run away from home. She was in a family situation that was unhealthy in a country that was unsafe and she fled. She went on to have a pretty good life. She did have strong emotions about the fact that she had left siblings behind, but the emotions were too much to fully process so she tossed them aside. Her subconscious mind, however, which is like the control center for her entire being, caught those neglected emotions and decided to help her out by processing the emotions for her. An elaborate guilt trip of physical pain ensued. The torment began like an alarm clock each month during her menstruation. Her subconscious mind had created a genius way of "properly punishing" her for leaving her siblings behind. While consciously she would never choose to feel the physical pain that took her down each month, subconsciously she felt she deserved it and, therefore, created it.

As soon as my client had conscious awareness of the racket her subconscious mind was running, a few things occurred as part of the chain reaction of her newfound understanding. First, the monthly suffering stopped. It could not continue because once a thing is known in consciousness it cannot be unknown. Since there was no more pain, her doctors were able to wean her off of the medication. The next thing that happened, of necessity, was that she had to feel the long buried emotions. This was tough.

The good news about feelings, however, is that they are not meant to be stagnant. They are fluid by nature. When you feel your feelings directly, they cannot help but transmute. They are moving, flowing life force energy. By feeling the depth of guilt and sorrow for what had happened, my client's feelings were able to return to what they really were which was energy. Once her energy was reclaimed and re-purposed, she was free. She went on to become a prolific artist and her works shed light on what was happening in that region of the world, thereby helping the masses.

This is what is possible when you let go of anything that blocks, hinders, or delays the flood gates of your creativity and inspiration. For me it meant learning to walk again. I had to train myself to walk with my head up. No more hiding out. No more lying low. This was new and uncomfortable territory. It meant being seen. Most of the time it is lovely to face the world, but facing the world also means coming eyeball to critical, judging eyeball with others.

I was recently getting ready to go up on stage for a speaking engagement and felt a woman eyeing my exposed legs. In truth, I was already self-conscious about the length of my dress with my bare legs, so her chastising gaze definitely penetrated. The more "on stage" I am in my life, the more judged I am by others. There are times when that feeling is almost enough to get me head down back in my cave. The thing is, though, once you have tasted freedom, once you have claimed your life's purpose—your joy, your beauty, your intelligence, your creativity—once you have said, *YES!* it is very hard to curl back up into a ball and play dead.

A magical thing happens when you triage leaking energy. When you are finally willing to detach from life's many diversions and focus fully on letting your life be a revelation, this is when you become a force to be reckoned with. Once I claimed my life and learned to walk with my head held high, I became more effective as a human being. I am more available for decisive, productive actions. As you allow old barriers in your life to come crashing down, you find yourself lit up like fire works with massive inspiration and the facility to bring it into manifested form.

For example, when I am no longer protecting or defending my little self, I am ripe for meaningful action. When I read that women in Afghanistan can have their fingers chopped off for wearing nail polish, all of the rage that exists within me galvanizes. All of the rage that I have ever known in my soul's entire existence; rage for every time I have ever been hurt or harmed, mutilated in my own way, that rage rises. It is compounded by the cellular rage I carry for every time any person throughout all of time has been abused or harmed. All of that rage gets the rally call of my soul. When I am clean and clear with my energy and have removed my own emotional and behavioral blockages, then I can take that rage and return it to what it really is—energy and passion. Gushing with intense passion, I am now free to take action. I can write about it. I can speak out about it. I can join organizations, write letters, *do* something. I can also take all of that energy, brew it up, and lay it out. I can take everything I am and lay my consciousness down upon any person, anywhere who hurts, harms, humiliates, dominates, objectifies, or bullies another.

I once heard a story about a career criminal. He had no idea that a group of people living far away had heard of his crimes and were praying for him. The criminal went off to work one day, to commit a robbery, but he couldn't. It made no sense to him. He wanted to. He planned to, but he was not physically able to follow through. There is a power to our thoughts. Yes, there must have been a place deep within the criminal that really did want to come clean in order for the prayers to work, that is true. Yet, the value of our connectedness cannot be denied. The place in me that is fed up with being harmed reaches across time and space into the place in another who is fed up with hurting and harming and all manner of possibility is born. Astrophysicists already know that if you wave your hand in one place it has ripple effects that extend to the farthest star. Your job is to galvanize your hurt and rage, transmute it back into its truest essence, which is passion, and then fire it off.

Shoot the best of you out into the world like a fiery arrow confident that it is sure to hit its mark!

As I do so, I know that somewhere there is a person who used to think it was okay to sell children into slavery or women into sex trafficking, or bully a kid on the playground, drop litter on the beach, dump chemicals in the ocean, sell crappy food, or run a political office for personal power rather than public gain—and right now, in this moment, I am knowing that they cannot. They simply cannot go about negative, harmful business-as-usual when your galvanized conscience rests heavy upon them. It is not possible when you choose to dis-allow the individual or systematic dehumanization of others. It will make no sense to the perpetrator. Perhaps the old criminal way of being is what they or their family have always done. Perhaps it is what lets them feel big enough or strong enough to face the day. I do not know. I do know that thought is power and that the tsunami of your focused energy is formidable, to be sure.

This is what happened on the eternal eighth day of our becoming. Every morning we awoke to God whispering a familiar song in our ears, *I have given you everything, baby. It is on you; do what you can do. I have given you everything, baby. It is on you; do what you can do...* We grew and expanded in our consciousness, learning how to create what we want and release what no longer serves us. Then, at some point along the way, we all fall into the swoon. Have you gotten your swoon on yet? Swooning is a moment when you are washed over with tremendous love. Love for life, for God, for everyone, and everything. The swoon is very much like a burst of inspiration, but it has an extra richness to it. Swooning is devotional. It is a flow state. It is inspiration on steroids. When you swoon, you feel intense love coupled with a deep yearning to live a devotional life, to give everything that you are to a higher purpose, greater cause. You can be carried away in an exquisite swoon by a song or moment of great art. Swooning can also occur for no reason at all.

I remember once when I was a teenager going through a break up with a boyfriend. I plopped myself down in the middle of my bedroom floor and sobbed uncontrollably, the ugly cry—tears, snot, and prehistoric animalistic noises coming out of me. I was inconsolable. I was a teenager going through a break up and I knew that I would never find true love again. And I didn't. At least not for another two or three weeks! But at some point in the middle of my meltdown I had an awakening. Even while I was devastated, I became simultaneously aware of the absolute rapture of life. I was wiping tears away with my sleeve and thinking, *My God. My God, how gorgeous life really is. How perfect life is.* I remember so clearly sitting on that bedroom floor at two o'clock in the morning feeling both heartbroken and utterly aware of the perfection of life. The swoon fills you with a desire to serve life, to give everything. It drops you deeply into a devotional practice. This was a turning point in my young life. I had gained the experiential awareness that I am part of some ecstatic eternal flow. I understood that life includes the tough stuff and the smooth sailing moments and that what is most critical is to capture the rapture and ride it, come what may. Simply, on the eighth day, we fell in love with God.

Just as you can do things to activate your indwelling source of inspiration, you can also learn to swoon on demand. The swoon fills you with love and inspiration and dives you deeply into that for which you were born. So, how do you swoon on demand? Actors, musicians, and athletes spend hours rehearsing and practicing the technical aspect of their craft. When it is show time or game time, however, all of that practice has to be tossed aside. Does it go anywhere? No, all of those drills and repetitions have become ingrained in their muscle memory. They have absorbed the practice and it is now part of them so they no longer need to think about the technical aspect of each move or gesture; they can focus fully on the present moment.

The same is true when you have a strong, consistent spiritual practice which includes regular moments of prayer—the kind of prayer that is not a begging beseeching prayer, but rather prayer that is in gratitude for that which you do have and that which is even now coming into fruition. Along with regular prayer, a strong spiritual practice includes meditation and visioning. I also include drinking lots of fresh, pure, clear, clean water and eating foods that are filled with life force and energy. Additionally, you want to make sure that you are regularly stretching and working out so that you have a strong, flexible physical temple to carry you through your life's journey. As you develop a lifestyle that becomes spiritual practice in motion, you are able to toss the conscious practice aside—does it go anywhere? No, it has become ingrained. Prayer and caring for yourself become reflexive. Food gets served and you bless it because what else would you do? With these practices in place as your infrastructure, you are free to swoon on demand.

You can simply look at yourself in the mirror and allow yourself to be washed over in love. Be overwhelmed by the gorgeousness of life. Look at yourself and say, *God really worked it out when she made me!* Imagine being audacious enough to look yourself straight in the mirror and proudly declare, *Use me Lord, because all of this (pointing to yourself) is just too fine to waste!!!!* Society can be quick to crush boldness and confidence, but what if you claimed the gift you were God given to give? What if you not only claimed it, but what if you walked out of your front door each day searching for every possible opportunity to shine and share it?

You get juicy when you let yourself live in the swoon. Life becomes engaging and delicious. It is consuming in the best possible way. You lay down at night utterly exhausted from the tip of your toes to the top of your head, aching with the best ever soreness of fully giving over to that thing for which you were born. Swooning is a deeper way of self-inspiring. It is about surrendering to your life's calling because there is an intense internal need to share your gifts. When you do, you start understanding how Mother Teresa could spend her whole life around a bunch of dirty, sick people, because that is not what she saw. She saw the dance of humanity, no victim, no savior, only our interconnectedness and the lifeline that we are for one another. We belong to each other. There is no other option. It is like the left leg trying to step forward and the right leg trying to go backward. They are connected; they need to work harmoniously. So too, it is with you and me.

Once you experience the swoon state, you understand how Dr. King could come in on a dream and give everything for it, including his life. It is because he had that wormhole moment when he was in one space-time continuum where things appeared set and unchangeable, but he went to the mountaintop. He saw life as it really is, that swoon of our real perfection. He saw that we really are the beloved community. We *can* get along and so much more than that. Can you find something to swoon for, something to give yourself over to?

That is what happened on the eternal eighth day of our becoming. Every day God whispers gently in your ear, *I have given you everything. It is on you. Do what you can do.* Day in and day out, you hear the call, until your last day. Are you living in a way that on your last day you can answer God by saying, *I gave YOU everything. I gave you the best of me. I gave you the worst of me. I gave you the blood, sweat, and bones of me. I gave you mountains of gratitude, oceans of devotion. I gave you the vast barren deserts of my heartbreaks and losses. I gave you the fertile fields of my wins and joys. I gave you my sons and my daughters, my consciousness, and my creativity. I gave it all up to you. All of those moments when I felt stranded at the doorstep of your presence and the moments I felt held in a way that would last forever. I gave you everything. I served life. I did life. I went off on life.* Can you say that? Are you living a life that will justify you saying such things? Are you living such a convicted life that no matter what voices of insanity surround you from time to time, whether on the news or in your home, you always know who and whose you are? Are you living a life where you can look out at all that you have created and *you* can say, *It is good.*

It will require something. It will mean something. It will mean breaking a sweat. It will mean driving past the fast food, dead food, drive through restaurants and going home and chopping up some vegetables. It will mean thinking your own thoughts, not the media's. It will mean being a stand for what is good and right and true. It means rising up, speaking out, fighting back, making a difference, being the difference. It means letting yourself swoon for God, letting yourself be washed over with the inspiration, passion, and desire to live devotionally, to give your whole self to this life so that when you roll up to Heaven's pearly gates, your gas tank is on empty, red light flashing. I want to show up so utterly well used that they will have to send an angel out with a gas can to put a few more drops of life force in me just to roll me inside! When I am done, I want to stop, drop, and crumble into nothing more than dust and bone and the memory of a good time. Are you with me on this? Can you join me? Will you?

There is a price. Your swoon comes at a cost. It means knowing that the creation story did not end on the seventh day. It did not stop with God kicking back in a La-Z-Boy and chugging a green drink while channel surfing. The story of creation continues right here, right now, with you. Everything you do, everything you say, and everything you think is recorded in the Book of All Times. It is like God said, *It's on you, baby. Do what you can do.* My good suggestion? Whatever you do, do it with a swoon. Do it with your heart and your guts, your passion and devotion, do it with everything you've got. Why? Because anything less is just marking time.

What makes you swoon? What do you care about? What consumes you? Are there causes that you feel drawn to? Could you choose to tithe part of your income toward a humanitarian organization you want to support, thereby making your business more compelling to others and filling you with deeper satisfaction at the same time? What makes life juicy and worth your while?

_____

_____

_____

_____

Now find a way to make sure this passion is addressed in some way on a weekly basis, perhaps daily. Make sure to schedule it in, even if that seems silly. For example, dance and nature are passions for me and yet there are times when weeks, even months, go by and I am not engaged in either. For me, it comes down to scheduling it into my week. Even if it means, ten minutes at home with music blasting while dancing in my living room. That can be just enough to get my blood flowing and inspiration pumping. What works for you? Now, schedule it in. Make a plan. Be accountable by telling someone else. Let your passions become part of the ultimate signature of your life. Your soul will thank you for it.

9

Mind Design...
Design Your Mind

Consider all of the information you have received thus far. Inspiration is a natural, organic, innate aspect of your physical, biological, psychological, and spiritual self. There is a call on your life. There is a gift you are meant to share. We first explored different tools you can use to help fine tune and clarify your life's calling. Then, we reviewed ways you can prime yourself for inspiration with regular daily practices that open you to your indwelling guidance. We also discussed the necessity of cleaning up any energy leaking habits or behaviors and choosing to live in the swoon, that devotional, inspired awareness of your oneness with God.

Now scan all of the different tools you can use to gain clarity regarding your brand of inspiration, from journaling and childhood hobbies to the adjectives you have gathered from various resources, to the insights and practices others use to awaken their inspiration. Sit with all of this information and then employ the Life Visioning Process to vision for your life's purpose.

Begin in meditation. Breathe. Relax. Center. Recall times in your life when you felt great happiness, easy, simple moments: a child's belly laugh, a walk in the woods, beholding a magnificent rainbow, waterfall, sunrise, or sunset. Let yourself wash over with gratitude. From this sweet place, ask yourself, "What is God's vision for my life?" Notice what comes up. You can write notes as you go along or wait until you have completed the process before making notes:

What is God's vision for my life?

_____

_____

_____

_____

After asking yourself each question, give ample time to allow guidance to come forth. You may receive your guidance in the form of sentences, words, pictures, feelings, smells, symbols, sounds, or direct knowing. However your guidance arrives is perfect. Simply allow responses to come forward after asking each question and then gently move on to the next:

What's Your What?

What gifts, qualities, and resources do I already have to help me realize God's vision for my life purpose?

_____

_____

_____

_____

Next: Is there anything I need to release or let go of in order to fully realize God's vision for my life purpose?

_____

_____

_____

Once again: What is God's greatest vision for my life?

_____

_____

Lastly: Return to gratitude. Flood yourself with gratitude for all that you already have: this breath, the vastness of the sky, a blade of grass. Continue calling forth all that you are grateful for until you become like a fountain gushing over with gratitude.

Now write a purpose statement for yourself. Why am I here? What is my purpose? Make it specific. If you are here to be a light upon the world, great! But be specific—what does that mean? It can be, "I am a light upon the world here to shine as a seventh grade math teacher." Or, "I am a light upon the world here to shine through my acting, writing, dancing, singing, painting, living, loving, parenting, business-building, serving..." How do you specifically shine in this world? What will you be doing when you are fully living the spark of inspiration you are God-intended to be? The behavior that you come up with may change; however, it is important to begin with a specific goal, action, or awareness. At the very center of all that I do or wish to do, what is my life's truest purpose?

For many years, I thought I would have a life unlived. I thought that the thing I was born for would go unrealized. I felt like my job was to lift everyone else up, help everyone else be successful. I regularly found myself at the side of famous, extraordinarily accomplished people, and I thought that my lot in life was to be the bystander, the wingman. Then one seemingly unremarkable phone conversation changed everything.

I reconnected with an artist I had known many years prior. When I met him, he was successful. When we reconnected years later, his stellar fame was worldwide. While we were speaking, even though I was doing well in my own endeavors, I found myself pulled down with that old feeling, *Here I am again on the periphery of someone else's greatness like a perennial cheerleader.* As we reflected on our earlier friendship, he said those magic words. He said something that reframed my whole existence. He said I had been a muse for him. At first, I found that insulting, but then awareness struck like a lightning bolt. That is the role I have played my whole life, the illuminator, the "waker-upper." Once I accepted my purpose and chose to flow with my life rather than view it as an insurmountable block in the way of my good, then I was free to be successful in my own right. This is the value of clarifying your "what," accepting it, and working with it.

Recall the qualities of God that have special resonance for you. List the top three:

1. _____

2. _____

3. _____

Visualize yourself doing your life's purpose while embodying these adjectives. Notice what kind of feeling tone you get. It should feel juicy and exciting. The process of visualizing can be a powerful way to activate your inspiration.

While your key qualities are beginning to come alive inside of you, it is time to court inspiration. Think of inspiration as a lady and treat her accordingly. Dress your environment to please her. For example, if you are a writer, let your writing area have symbols and images that awaken your creative juices. I have the good fortune of coaching several New York Times best-selling authors. With each one, we have taken time to consider how they can create the most compelling work environment possible—using colors, music, lighting, quotations, artwork, and even aroma. Consider every aspect of your work/play environment. Keep a list of the top three adjectives/qualities that personify you nearby so that you are regularly reminded of the unique way that you are here to shine. Have your life purpose statement written out and beautifully, prominently displayed. Play conducive music, keep fresh flowers, plants, or perhaps a water fountain. Become sensitive to what sparks you, what creates a sense of flow and prosperity for you. Strategically place these items or symbols of them around your work area. In this way, you let external stimuli initiate your daily awakening. Take a moment now to consider what elements would enhance your creative space:

Colors: _____

Quotes: _____

What's Your What?

Pictures: _____

Art/Special Pieces: _____

Music: _____

Lighting: _____

Alter/Sacred Area: _____

Scents: _____

Set aside some time purely devoted to infusing your creative area with conscious content. Begin by straightening up. Release clutter. Establish order. Then, allow your creativity to have full sway as you fill your environment with the essence of who you really are. Inspiration is about arousing specific emotions or actions. An effective environment can create the perfect state for igniting inspiration. Your environment stimulates chemical responses within you. When your environment is pleasing and conducive, it awakens your indwelling syntropic impulse and starts pushing the waters about. Just the right song or photograph can get those waves rolling and before you know it, you are surfing on a beautiful flow state, sailing in the zone.

This is what President Barack Obama did when he took his jogs along the Mall in Washington, D.C. He gave his body the physical task of running at a methodical, rhythmic pace, which created a light hypnotic trance state. Once his mind entered this altered state of consciousness, he flooded it with symbols and images of his deepest yearnings: Symbols of freedom, collaboration, working together, struggling together, fighting together, and overcoming together. All of the great monuments and historic landmarks that he passed along his "simple jog" seeped deeply into his subconscious. He created the perfect opportunity to be physically, psychologically, and emotionally available for the unleashing of massive inspiration and desire. This is what we can do. This is what you must do. Most people just happen upon that lucky equation by accident. You have the power to self-initiate, to spark inspiration purposely. The power is within your reach.

When you dress your environment and place yourself in locations that thrill you and send you, places that remind you of the purity of your heart's desire, you set yourself up for full realization. Every cell in your body gushing with activating hormones, renewing energy. From this place, all things are possible.

Right where you are, right now, all things are possible. *Breathe in this truth. Right here, right now, I am connected to an endless, fathomless, supreme source of dynamic good. In this moment, I allow myself to become open and available. I say yes to flow. I say yes to prosperity. I say yes to joy and happiness and contentment. I say yes. Breathe in your yes. Breathe in your yes all the way down to your smallest toe, up your legs, pelvis, genitals, belly, back, arms, shoulders, neck, and head. And so it is. Yes!*

What's Your What?

I remember sitting in Rev. Michael Bernard Beckwith's office one time. I was there upholding my position as a practitioner. Agape Practitioners are individuals who have spent a number of years in class studying and practicing the art and science of prayer, a very active, affirmative, trans-denomenational (inclusive of all religions), dynamic kind of prayer. One of the honors we share is that we take turns meeting in Rev. Michael's office before each service so that we can set the tone. Our job is to know with conscious conviction that everyone who hears the word spoken that day, whether live at Agape in Los Angeles or streaming from around the world, gets exactly what they most need at that time.

One Wednesday evening, I was sitting in Rev. Michael's office, deep in prayer, when Rhonda Brittan, the guest speaker for that evening, walked in. I greeted her and she came over and sat next to me on a little, two-seater couch. As we sat side by side, I closed my eyes and went back into prayer. I held in my consciousness a certainty that all was well for her and that her talk would have a mighty impact. As I prayed, I became aware of a low dull ache in my gut and a heaviness in my heart spreading through my chest. I know that disease often starts with dis-ease in the form of imploded emotions, emotions held within, so I took a moment to assess what was happening inside of me.

I realized that the pain in my body was the painful awareness that I would never sit in her seat. So close, we were side by side, but I realized I would never sit where she sits. I would never be the

Julie Moret

one going out to give the main talk. I was back in my "wingman" mentality, thinking I would always be back-up support, never the one experiencing that prime, front and center, main stage real estate. I had good reasons for feeling that way. It seems people often have good arguments to coddle their excuses for giving up or quitting. I was not a minister at the time. I did not have a best-selling book at the time, and I was not on a television show. I did not have the standard criteria to get front and center as a guest speaker. The pain I was feeling was the pain of a life unlived. I felt that something I was built for, something that seemed to choose me beyond any kind of conscious vocational choice on my part, a seed, a need placed deeply within me, was not possible.

Have you ever felt that way? You know there is something that is for you, but it seems too far away, impossible, or elusive. It is not necessarily something that you have ambition for; it is more like a soul congruency. In a sense, I was just sitting there feeling sorry for myself because I knew that my soul's calling would go unanswered in my lifetime.

The story could end right there. How many times has the story stopped there, a hope or dream stashed away in the could've, would've, should've pile? This is why you have to stay on the ache, on the "what" of your life. What are you meant for, what do you crave, what are you drawn to, what do you desire? What is your what? This is the worthy question. What is your what? You must stay on your what, because often times, the how is just not possible!

That takes us back to the top. What is your what? What is your dream? We know who we are and what we are here for. Sometimes it may get a bit fuzzy or unclear. But, ultimately, we know who we are. I have worked with hundreds of people in a counseling setting and am clear, we all come in on a dream, and deep down we know what it is.

We have all been there. That knowing that lives inside of you, that knows with utter certainty you are born of greatness. It is your divine inheritance. Then the question of "how" pops up and it seems a far cry. This is why I now follow the advice of international author and prosperity teacher, Edwene Gaines. She says not to waste a second worrying about the "how." How is up to God. Your job is to live in the conviction of your good. Your job is to create inspiration-rich environments and opportunities. Your job is to light yourself up with the presence of God and let God handle the how.

That is the way you do the work. You gain the intellectual under-standing that inspiration is an innate aspect of your biological, physiological, psychological, spiritual self. You use your tools to gain clarity regarding your particular brand of inspiration, the way in which you are here to hold up your end of luminosity on the planet, and you utilize your practical, daily tools to spark inspiration on a regular basis. To be clear, the inspiration we speak of is not explosive desire or energy for the sake of bluster or busyness. True inspiration impacts society. It shifts the course of humanity. It makes us wiser. It makes us better, deeper, richer. True inspiration is universal and archetypal. There is a special kind of wisdom that happens when you are, at last, willing to be your true self. In *The Republic*, Plato called this occurrence the "molding of oneself" that results from an intense desire to be "of the whole."

Can you be that raw? Can you let yourself be dropped to your knees, crushed to your core with the desire for full self-revelation? Are you willing to live like the bumblebee? One sting and you are gone. One life. One full tilt, full lived, used up until you are nothing more than dust on the floor, life. Never in my wildest dreams could I have imagined that I would be a regular, front and center, main stage public speaker, but here I am. I am fully living beyond my dreams. Inspiration is the way in. Inspiration is the way out. Sit quietly. Let her whisper in your ear. You are meant to illumine the skies with your unique gift. Let inspiration guide you home. Let her wrap herself around you so that you become re-fleshed bone, made new in this moment. Born whole. Born willing.

Breathe in fully. Let yourself be inspired, literally "breathed in." May you be oxygenated by the breath of God this very day. I am willing for life. I am available. I am pliable in God's hand. I am grateful and thankful for the Absolute Inspiration that thrives in me this day, and I know that, truly, all is well.

10

When Life Gives You Lemon Drops, Grab Them!

You now have clarity about what you want and how you are meant to shine in this world. You also know how to coax your own indwelling source of inspiration to help catapult you into fulfilling your life's purpose. But what does it take to actually grasp your good? We live in such a wanting, craving, longing after, coveting-what-others-have kind of society. The amped-up pace of life becomes a set-up loop because there is always a faster, better, newer model; as soon as you get what you want, the next shiny new thing is already on deck tarnishing the glow of the current win. We find ourselves like mice running round and round on an exercise wheel, racing faster and faster, going nowhere and getting nothing but exhausted!

It is time to chart a new course, to follow soul desires and feel what it feels like to have a true want, wish, or desire, carry it through to the finish line, and then *enjoy* it. It is time to grasp your good and savor it. Why? Because unconscious patterns derived from family, society, or culture often impede our ability to not only obtain our good, but also prevent us from savoring it. It does not matter where the patterns come from. What matters is that they become insidiously ingrained in our thinking and can become the very thing that lets a person get close to that which they desire, but somehow it seems to slip away. Often, these patterns get set up quite early on in life.

For example, a few years ago my son and I were in Reverend Kathleen McNamara's office at the Agape International Spiritual Center where I work. She offered my son a lemon drop and my son, in his shyness, pressed back against my legs and shook his head, no. That was fine, I finished my conversation with Kathleen and then she went on about her business and we went on about ours. When my son and I got outside of the building, he used his pointer finger to motion me down close to his face. I leaned down and he whispered, "I really do want a lemon drop." Why on earth does that happen in life? He was right there. He could have gone both fists in on that lemon drop jar. It was right within his reach, but he let the moment pass him by.

Has that ever happened to you? Of course it has! It is not a question of whether it has happened, but how many times? You are just about to meet the guy, kiss the girl, win the race, get the job, or have the behind you know you are God-intended to have. You are so close to grasping that which you know is yours and yet, somehow, the moment seems to slip away. I remember several years ago, I was living in New York City and the movie *The Princess Bride* came on television. As I watched it, I was filled with joy from Mandy Patinkin's performance. He played Inigo Montoya and all through the movie his character kept reciting, "My name is Inigo Montoya. You killed my father, prepare to die!" It seemed to me that he was having the time of his life playing that character.

I found myself almost compulsively thinking about his funny performance. Then, there I was one day, walking down Broadway in New York City and out of the corner of my eye, I noticed Mandy Patinkin walking right beside me, Inigo Montoya himself! I remember so clearly thinking what a wonderful life we are living. What a fun, funny, humorous, perfect life. Here I had been thinking about this person and his delightful, inspired performance and all of a sudden he was twelve inches from me. Fantastic!

I felt so happy that I had the opportunity to thank him for his performance that I immediately began to practice. I began practicing in my mind how I was going to say thank you to the person walking right next to me. Why? Because I did not want to sound dumb. I did not want to appear foolish. I wanted to make sure I got it right. Ever been there? So close to a sweet moment and then stalled out because of insecurities, self-consciousness, or the need to be perfect?

So, there we were, walking down Broadway. In my mind, we were walking down Broadway together, but in actuality he had no idea I even existed. We were in a sea of hundreds of rushing- about New Yorkers. I kept practicing in my mind what I should say to him. Maybe, *Excuse me Sir, are you Mr. Mandy Patinkin?* Or, I could go for cute, like, *My name is Inigo Montoya, you killed my father, prepare to die!* I continued sorting through the possibilities as we came to the end of the first block. Being New Yorkers, we all energetically dared the taxicabs to hit us as we crossed the street en masse without looking. We survived. We made it to the other side of the street, and then Mandy and I, and a few hundred other people, continued walking down the next block.

Finally, I got it. I knew exactly what I wanted to say. I felt comfortable. I felt like I had it just right. It was perfect and I could not wait for my big moment. We got to the end of the second block. I stopped and turned to my right to thank him. He stopped and turned to *his* right and disappeared in a crowd of people down a busy side street. All I could do was stand there on that bustling New York City street corner. I stood there getting bumped and jostled by all of the rushing about New Yorkers. I stood there and cried like a baby.

Have you ever felt so cheated by life? Ever gotten so close to something so sweet only to have it slip away? As I stood there on that street corner, I realized that I needed something. For me to get through this life, for me to survive this life, much less thrive in it, I needed something. I needed some tools. I needed some truths. I needed something I could trust. I needed something I could have faith in, something I could lean into when the world feels topsy-turvy and upside down. What came to me are three basic universal truths, three laws you can call upon at a moment's notice and let them be your respite in the storm. With these laws tucked safely in your back pocket, you will always have fertile ground for inspiration to take root.

The first law is that you live in a responsive universe. What does that mean? It means that your thoughts backed by emotion impact the circumstances and experiences of your life. It is as though you live in the land of Play-Doh. Not Plato, the deep and meaningful philosopher, but Play-Doh as in the clay-like stuff that comes in small plastic canisters. You can take out a great big hunk of clay and mold it and shape it and make all kinds of wonderful creations. Your thoughts are the same way. When you have a strong thought backed by passionate emotion, it goes out into higher conscious- ness and molds and shapes the experiences of your life.

This basic tenet easily rolls us into the second law which is the "good news, bad news" law that you live in an objective universe. This means that the universe mirrors back to you at the level of your thoughts, beliefs, patterns, and decisions. The universe mir- rors back your conscious thoughts and the unconscious ones. In a nutshell, your life responds to all of your thoughts, the good ones, and the other ones!

You can take a great big hunk of clay and shape it and mold it and make something magnificent like a castle with turrets and even a moat. But, if you neglect your clay, if you leave it out in your front lawn to weather and age and be trampled on by yourself and others, pretty soon it is just going to look like a great big pile of poop. That is exactly what your unattended thoughts are like, and

I promise you, nobody wants to be walking behind the steaming piles of unconscious thoughts you are dropping!

The good news about living in an objective universe is that this is the law that helps you develop a spiritual practice. It becomes clear that you must gain dominion over your thoughts and the best way to do that is through daily spiritual practice. Meditation, prayer, and visioning are all powerful ways to get back in the driver's seat of your consciousness so that you may use the power of your mind to help you create more of what you *do* want and less of what you do not want.

The third universal principle has become my life's mantra. This is the law that you can fully rest in now. This law declares that you live in a gracious universe. Feel how good that feels. *I live in a gracious universe.* Breathe that awareness into your heart and mind, into every organ, action, and function within your being. It is like you can take a warm bubble bath or a sweet afternoon nap and know that everything is going to be all right. Your life has your back, and all is well.

Knowing that this is so, we can dive in and explore this principle a bit further. You live in a gracious universe. This means that your life is constantly, consistently erring on the side of your good. I say this gently and with great care because I know that we have all been through challenges. We have all had struggles. Some people may be experiencing certain challenges right now that certainly do not feel like life is erring on the side of their good. What I mean is that ultimately, your life is for you. You were born with a renewable spirit. This is a remarkable trait that you have inherited. It is extraordinary.

Over the years, I have counseled hundreds of people, thousands including seminars and workshops. Many of those people lived through unimaginable circumstances. It continues to amaze me how some of them have been able to attribute a meaning and a value to those undesired experiences that raised them higher than they could have ever imagined possible. This is a facility that is within our psychological makeup. You are renewable. Your heart is renewable. You can find love again. You can know wholeness again. You can enjoy dynamic prosperity again. You can be fully creative again. And, if you never experienced those things to begin with, you can claim them now! What a gift to be self-renewing.

Ultimately, this means you have the ability to self-inspire. How? Make a choice. Choose to accept the high calling placed upon your life, and trust that there is one even if you cannot feel it in this moment. It is your job to develop a faith, an absolute trust that you are not wasted matter. You are here on point and it is your responsibility to live in the conviction that there is good here for you and that you are here for good. Your job is to trust life and let your faith lead the way. It will.

That all sounds good, but how does it actually work? Your life is on a constant feedback loop. It is ever circling back around to offer you up your good. It is like you are in a fabulous restaurant and the five star waiter keeps returning over and over again offering you that which you desire. Are you ready yet? Can you accept it now? Can you handle it? Would you like an appetizer or are you ready for the whole enchilada? This feedback loop keeps cycling back around waiting for your willingness.

Now, if you did not get the lead in your high school class play and you feel that loss derailed the rest of your life, does it mean that all of a sudden your twenty, thirty, forty, fifty, sixty, seventy, eighty year old self is going to be walking down the street one day and the drama coach from the local school across the way is going to spot you from her window and call out, "You, you are the one! You must be the lead in our next production of Oklahoma!" No. Not likely.

What it means is that you can ask yourself what quality you thought you would experience by getting the lead in the class play. Qualities of God are peace, love, joy, prosperity, abundance, freedom, creativity, happiness, trust, faith, justice, etcetera. Think about the quality you expected to experience if you had gotten the lead in the class play, met the guy, kissed the girl, won the race, gotten the job, or whatever moment you feel slipped away from you. What quality do you believe you would have gained had it gone the way you thought you wanted it to?

Now, your job is to flood your life with that quality. Find pictures, images, songs, smells, tastes, activities, and anything else that awakens that quality within you. Dress your environment with this quality. Adorn your daily activities with this quality. Then watch as the responsive universe that you live in replies, *Oh, she is all about prosperity now. Oh, he is opening up to dynamic creativity. Oh, love is what we are doing now.* Because you live in a responsive, objective universe, the universe will then say, *I see. I thought we were doing misery, lack, despair, and victimhood, but now I realize we are going full tilt into love, joy, wholeness, prosperity, and creativity. Great, I'm on it!* The universe pulls a hard right turn and begins to reflect back people, places, and events at the level of your newly claimed good.

Once you begin this practice, a whole new world opens up for you and you find yourself swimming in the flow of life rather than against it. Mystical, awe-inspiring events and circumstances become your new normal. For example, months after the initial lemon drop incident of late 2011, I was driving my son home from school one day when I heard him call out from the back seat, "I want to go to Agape." Now, Agape is my spiritual home. I am thrilled that my son wants to be there. However, as I fully explained to him, there was absolutely no conceivable way that we could go to Agape that day. Not only had he already been to school, but he had a play date as well. So, obviously, the only choice for me was to race home, throw supper on the table, run him upstairs so we could hurry up and have our slow down relaxation time, and then dump him into bed so we could get back on schedule!

After I rationally explained this to my child, he answered me with silence. A few quiet minutes passed as I raced our car down the street rushing toward home. Then, a little louder, I heard, "I WANT TO GO TO AGAPE." There was nothing on earth that was going to change my mind at that point because I definitely needed to get my kid home; however, I am not so dense or so rigid that I did not notice a little something behind his plea. So I asked my son why he wanted to go to Agape. Silence. A few moments passed and then loud and clear as a bell, he declared, "I want a lemon drop!"

This was remarkable. There had not been one mention of lemon drops since that initial lemon drop incident several weeks prior. I told my son I would be happy to take him to Agape another time and proceeded on towards home. He sat silent in the back seat of our car, but I could feel him energetically pressing in on me. It was when I pulled into our garage and parked my car that I heard the voice. Not my son's voice. Not my voice. The Voice, that soul calling that lives inside of you, that beckons you, that urges you on to fulfill your greatest heart's desire. I heard that voice within me and it said, *Are you kidding? You have a human being on fire in the back seat and all you are worried about is your schedule?* Quite frankly, all I could think was, *Yes, I really am concerned about my schedule.* As a mom, I live by the schedule. But the voice in my gut was louder than the one in my mind and so even though I was annoyed, I backed out of the garage and headed over to Agape.

However, I am a good mother and my job is to protect my child, so I spent the entire drive over to Agape explaining to my child all of the ways in which his plan was doomed for failure. Ever had that happen? Ever been right on the cliff of your greatest dream, ready to take flight when the people around you, the people who love you the most try to talk you down? They are trying to keep you safe and make sure you do not get hurt when everything inside of you is screaming, *Yes! This is my moment. This is my time. Jump! Jump!*

What's Your What?

Jump! Have you ever had someone try to tame you when you are ready to run free? Have you ever done that to yourself?

That is exactly what I did to my child. The whole car ride over to Agape, I explained to him all of the good reasons why his plan would never work: It was late. Kathleen might not even be at Agape anymore and even if she was still at Agape, she might not be in her office. But if she was at Agape and she was in her office, then most certainly she would be facilitating a practitioner counseling session and still not be available for us. However, if she was at Agape and she was in her office and she was not doing a practitioner session, then who was to say that she still had lemon drops? The last time we were there was months ago and that lemon drop jar was pretty low back then. But if she was at Agape and she was in her office and she was not doing a practitioner session and she did have lemon drops, why on earth would she offer one to my kid, because the last time he said no!

Here is where it is time to take a page from the child. That entire car ride over to Agape, my son did not pay one bit of attention to me. He was laser focused, eye on the prize. All he was thinking about was lemon drops. If he had any sideways thoughts at all, I am sure that he just wished the lady in the driver's seat would shut up! He probably wished he were in a taxicab and could just close the partition windows to block out all of my negativity. Can you do that? Can you be full speed racing towards your heart's desire and remain so convicted and focused that nobody, no matter how ill- or well-meaning, can talk you down? Can you keep yourself rooted in such a powerful way that other people's thoughts and opinions, even your own negative thoughts and opinions, just bead up and wick away like a great spiritual repellent?

When we pulled into the parking lot at Agape, my son jumped out of the car and raced up to Kathleen's window from the outside of the building. He cupped his hands to the window and peered inside before calling out, "She's not there." Again, I am a good mother. My job is to catch my kid when he falls, so immediately I kicked into mommy-mode, "Okay, sweetie, we can go into the bookstore and read one story before we head back home for supper." I thought that was quite magnanimous of me given my almost hysterical desire to get us back on schedule!

My son never heard a word I said. Instead, he raced around to the front of the building and flung open the great big entrance doors. We stepped into the main hallway. It was completely empty. Not a single person in sight. Now, here is something that nobody knows about Kathleen McNamara. People just think of her as heading up the practitioner core and being Michael Beckwith's long time right-hand person, but what most people do not know is that she can materialize. The hallway was completely empty and then all of a sudden, BAM! There she was, Kathy Mac, in the house!

This may sound like we are poised for the perfect happy ending, but please recall that the initial lemon drop incident of late 2011, occurred in Kathleen's office where those neon, lemony, yellow balls could not help but make her offer them up. We were now in the main hallway of Agape with no sign of lemon drops anywhere to make her even remotely think of sharing them. Additionally, her arms were laden with books and papers, which meant that clearly she was rushing out the door to go do very important things with very important people and certainly she did not have any time for us. Have you ever given yourself that head-trip? Ever told yourself you are not important enough for someone's time, energy, or love? Additionally, even if Kathleen was walking around ruminating over lemon drops all day, and even if she did have time for us, why on earth would she offer my son a lemon drop when he said no the first time!

I had barely gotten 'Hello' out of my mouth when Kathy Mac completely blew me off, turned to my son, and said, "Would you like a lemon drop?" "Yes!" he quickly answered, and off they went. I had to run down the hall to catch up with them. The administering of the lemon drop was like a high Japanese tea ceremony. She delicately raised the crystal goblet. My son gingerly extracted a shiny, sugary, ball, and he got his moment!

This is the life you are living. It is ever looping back around offering you a seat at the table of your own soul's divinity. You can have your moment now. Even if you feel that a million of them have passed you by, there is still one bright, shiny moment with your name on it. Are you ready for it? Can you handle it? Truly, your moment wants you. It wants your YES!

Like that time I was left standing abandoned and alone on that New York City street corner, it took me a while to put together some laws that I could count on, some principles I could have faith in when life gets out of whack. Then, there I was in my rat-infested New York City apartment one day. I called downstairs to the restaurant below me and ordered my lunch as I had done for as long as I had lived there. A few minutes later, I went to pick up my food. I walked all the way to the back of the cavernous, block long, completely empty restaurant to pay for my meal. Just as I was getting my money from my wallet, I noticed out of the corner of my eye that seated alone at a very large table, was Mandy Patinkin—Inigo Montoya himself! Not only was he sitting at a very large table by himself, he was sitting at the very large table by himself looking up at me, smiling. Not only was Inigo Montoya looking up and smiling at me, but he raised his hand to offer me a seat, and I got my moment!

That is your life. That is the nature and possibility of the life you are living. Whatever you want, whatever you need, it is always one solid prayer-backed-by-emotion away. A thought grounded in conviction, rooted in passion, this is the way towards grasping your good. Your impassioned soul-led desire is undeniable to the universe. It cannot help but respond in like measure to the intensity of that which you claim for yourself.

We take a moment to recall that the universe is unbiased in its response. It is objective and responds accordingly. We rest in the awareness that you live in a gracious universe. It is ever circling back around to provide for you the qualities of God that you most desire. Peace, prosperity, love, joy, creativity, order, wholeness,

freedom, divine right employment, divine right partnership. It is God's good wish to give you that which you desire.

Your good may come dressed exactly as you dreamt, or it may show up differently. That is the five-year story of my relationship with my husband. For five years he was right in front of me and I was like, *Excuse me, sir, can you just step aside, please. I am looking for a husband here. If you could just move over, I am trying to find a husband.* Finally, one day I looked at my man, and it was like, *Well alright!* The lights had suddenly come on and I got it. He was the one I was looking for! It is not for us to concern ourselves with the how, how it all should look or happen or how the inspiration will come. Yes, it is good to have a flexible idea; however, what matters most is simply that you develop a faith, a trust, an absolute knowing, that your life is for you. Truly, your life is for you, and all is well.

11

The Road to Mecca: Finding Home Along Your Way and Creating Inspiration in the Dailiness

Once you develop the energy, willingness, trust, and technology to go for the big things you most want, the next step is finding wonder, magic, and inspiration in the simple dailiness of life. Every year millions of people travel to Mecca, the holy land, to honor their spiritual convictions. Each aspect of their journey is full and complex. As daunting as it can be to prepare for the adventure of a lifetime, it is equally important to fully accept and appreciate the moment of actually making it to Mecca. This beckons a critical question, what do you do when your biggest dream, your greatest longing, finally comes true. Can you handle it? What comes next?

Considering the breadth of this fantastical journey to Mecca,

I began to wonder what it would be like if we all decided that our lives are a pilgrimage. A pilgrimage is a sacred journey with a holy destination. Can you imagine wearing that mantle? Can you imagine what your life would feel like to you if you woke each morning ready to set out on your sacred journey for the day? What a different feel that has from the dreary status quo of dragging along and merely clocking in and clocking out on the time card of life. What a difference from the full on declaration, *My life is a sacred journey with a holy destination!*

Imagine being out and about one day. You bump into an old friend and exchange basic pleasantries. "Hey, how are you doing? What are you up to?" The friend says something typical like, "Oh, I have to go to the store. I ran out of my old stuff. Gotta get some new stuff to go with my other stuff. What are you doing?" You simply smile and say, "I'm on a sacred journey with a holy destination." Imagine how dumbfounded your friend would be. "What?!" Talk about a paradigm shift. Your friend barely sputters out the question, "You are what?" Easy as pie you reply, "I am on a sacred journey with a holy destination. See ya!" And off you go, clear and committed to your fullest revelation, not only raising the bar on your life, but raising it for those around you as well.

If you were to do this, if you were to declare that your life is a sacred journey with a holy destination, the first step is to ask yourself, *How do I begin?* All great journeys begin in consciousness, in thoughts backed by feelings. Begin by identifying the quality that you would like your life's journey to embody, not just the goal at hand. What are the over-arching characteristics of your life, the driving feeling-tone? This is a perfect way to jump-start your own indwelling source of inspiration.

We all contain each of the qualities of God. You have within you peace, love, joy, prosperity, abundance, creativity, integrity, justice, and freedom. While you have these qualities, it is important to identify which ones inspire you—this is the beginning point in the sacred journey of an innovative, fulfilling life. Usually there are one or two qualities that resonate the most. Typically, they will have much to do with the ultimate signature of your life's story. Once identified, as we discussed in the previous chapter, you can use these God qualities to pump inspiration into your life experiences in such a dynamic way that one dose of inspiration begets another and another until you are thriving in an avalanche of awakened, inspired desire.

The process of identifying these qualities begins with awareness. As I reflect upon my life, I remember resonating with certain qualities from a young age. When I was a teenager, I spent hours running every day. I put in hours of running time for the rare exquisite ecstasy of the runner's high. While sometimes that euphoric state only lasted a second or two, that feeling was my driving force. As I look further back, I realize that I craved that feeling even earlier in my life when my family went boating and I would sit on the bow holding the railing as we raced across the ocean, hair flying, wind whipping. Even earlier as a young child, I remember that I could not wait to go to bed at night because I would astral travel high above the red clay mountains of Georgia. I felt so free, powerful, and happy soaring above the tree tops. In each case, that sense of absolute freedom was what compelled me. It was the passion that inspired me to fly higher, jump farther, run faster. It is the underlying quality that drives me still to this day.

We have already explored from various angles your main driving qualities. Like peeling back layers of an onion, take a moment and consider your through-line qualities, those guiding qualities that have propelled you forward from your earliest memories. Reflect on these qualities that compel you towards action and satisfaction and then list them below:

1. _____

2. _____

3. _____

Look back on your life and notice how you have often, usually un-consciously, found ways to surround yourself with these qualities. Perhaps there is one particular quality that especially stands out. Take a moment to recount all the times your abiding quality has been with you:

_____

_____

_____

Imagine how you can juice your life with this quality right now. Flood your home, office, even your car with pictures, images, symbols, sounds, tastes, smells, activities, colors, anything and everything that reminds you of your guiding qualities and awakens them within you.

For example, if peace is your charge in this lifetime, you could place pictures in your office, bedroom, car, and work area that remind you of this quality. This invites that level of peace to expand and multiply in your daily experiences. In this way, you become a self-inspiring individual truly capable of fulfilling your life's purpose. I suggest that you stop in this moment. Put this book down and go find one item to adorn your environment. Find one thing—a picture, word, phrase, symbol, something from nature, a special object—anything that reminds you of your core quality, and place it strategically in your environment. I assure you that this one, simple act will pay wondrous dividends.

Once identified, your main driving qualities become like a lighthouse beaconing to the world that this is who you are and what you stand for. Your true radiance flashes out into the universe vectoring all manner of like good back to you. What a powerful way to consciously travel through the course of your life. Once you decide to treat your life as a sacred journey, the next step is to ask yourself, *How am I packing for my travels? Do I have too much baggage?*

Shortly after my son was born, my husband and I decided to take him on an airplane ride to meet his great grandfather. I will always recall the image of my husband moving through the Los Angeles airport looking like a Sherpa in the Himalayan Mountains. He had a luggage cart piled high with suitcase after suitcase after baby bouncer, baby stroller, baby seat, baby ball. We were only going away for two days, but we brought everything we could think of because our Mecca of the moment was a good night's sleep. We brought every bit of baby gear we had in the hopes that something would work and we would get some sleep. Did we make it to our holy land of a good night's sleep? No, and we just about ruined the trip because we were so over burdened with stuff!

The question is, do you have too much baggage? Baggage can look many different ways, bitterness, anxieties, stresses, tensions, angers, resentments, jealousies, excess weight, or material things. As you scan your life, ask yourself, *Is it time to lay something down? Is it time to let something go?* How good would it feel, how much more energy would you have access to if you energetically, emotionally, and physically let something go right now. Imagine how much inspiration could flow freely through you if you uncluttered some aspect of your life. Take a breath. What can you lay down right now? What would make you freer, lighter, and happier, if only you would drop it right now?

_____

_____

I choose to let go. I choose to lay anything unwanted at the altar of my consciousness so that it may be returned to its original nature, which is energy. In this moment, I reclaim my full energy. I take back my whole self. I allow any fragmented aspects of myself to mend and release anything that does not serve my glory-bound self. I let it go now. Even if they were wrong and I was right, I let it go. Even if they hurt me, I let it go. Even if it was not fair, I let it go. I let him go. I let her go. I let go now. I let go to save my life. I let go to breathe in fresh new energy. I let go to get back my full self. I release anything that was a drain on my energy and I claim vitality. I claim joy. I claim freedom. I release all else in this moment and stand grateful for my flexible nature and willingness to move forward unloosed from my history.

While releasing excess baggage is good, you also want to ask yourself if there are any areas in your life where you do not have enough baggage. Every time my husband and I travel, that poor man ends up shirtless and sockless. Why? Because I have a fundamental inability to pack t-shirts and athletic socks. I can pack inappropriately high-heeled shoes until the cows come home, but t-shirts and athletic socks? Not on my radar. So love and basic necessity dictate that my husband now has to either pack double socks and t-shirts or go sockless and shirtless when we travel.

Ask yourself, are there any areas in your life where you are not taking care of yourself well enough and are therefore not only draining yourself, but draining those around you as well? Become aware of how you can better fortify yourself. How can you take better care of yourself and keep yourself better prepared and available for your good? Make these adjustments and notice how the universe responds accordingly. As you love yourself more and tend to yourself better, the responsive universe that you live in receives your intention and draws unto you people, places, and circumstances that mirror back your heightened level of self-care.

Now consider how you are doing in your day-to-day travels. How well do you attend to yourself? Do you take time to breathe and rest? Do you have a daily practice that nurtures and supports that which you desire to manifest in your life? For example, if you want to meet someone and enjoy a loving relationship with a wonderful partner, we can assume you will not be walking around with your hair up in a scrunchie all the time, wearing dirty sweats. You would want to attend to your basic hygiene and make sure you put yourself together in an appealing way.

If you are a musician, whether your Mecca is Carnegie Hall or Madison Square Garden, I trust you will spend time each day practicing your instrument. If what you desire is a deeper, more intimate connection with God, then you will probably meditate and create sacred moments for prayer and visioning. If what you desire is the healthiest, most dynamic life you can possibly live, then you will drink lots of fresh, pure, clear, clean water every day and eat foods filled with life, energy, and vitality. You will create time to move your body and get your circulation going. You will take time to stretch, knowing that in some cultures a person's age is based on the amount of flexibility in their spine. The more flexible your spine, the more flexible your mind will be, which allows you to more easily maneuver through life's various challenges and circumstances.

Why spend so much time attending to how you conduct yourself along your journey's way? Because sometimes the journey is all you get. Get that? Sometimes the journey is all you get. Reverend Dr. Martin Luther King Jr. was on an intellectual pilgrimage for nonviolence. Did he make it to the absolute Mecca of his heart's desire and experience complete peace and harmony in his lifetime? No. Did it matter? For him personally, no, and he knew it. He said in his *I've Been to the Mountaintop* speech on April 3, 1968, "…it really doesn't matter with me now." Why? Because he had been to the mountaintop. Dr. King went to the mountaintop of his heart's desire every single day. Every day he went to that place inside himself that knew beyond a shadow of a doubt that we can work it out. Every day he went to the mountaintop of his soul's desire. He lived there. He dwelled there. He knew we could learn to get along. He knew we could learn to behave ourselves, and more than that, he knew that we could learn to respect one another, love one another, and have compassion and kindness. Can you do that? Can you go to the mountaintop of your soul's desire in such a powerful, dynamic way every single day that the entire universe has to get up off of its lethargic axis just to meet you where you live?

Then, what? What happens when you do make it to Mecca? What happens when you stand for something, when you fight for something, when you give your all for something? What happens when, at last, you reach your heart's desire? Can you handle it? Can you receive your good? Can you train yourself for success, not just achieving it, but enjoying it, embodying it, and letting yourself use it as a spring board for greater good?

I remember reaching a point in my life when I was living my dreams and all of a sudden I noticed old, unhealthy relationships from earlier times popping up. People started coming around. I felt like I was living the crab in the bucket syndrome. The bigger I dreamed, the more in my zone I got, the more it felt like people were trying to pull me back down. Most with good intentions, they did not want me to get hurt or risk failing, or stand out too much. Whether their actions came from love or fear, it did not matter. All I knew was that I was done. Not another moment more could I sacrifice my radiance for someone else's comfort.

At first, I felt like a master martial artist blocking and parrying away those who would try to pull me back down to perceived safety and stifling normalcy. After some time, these feelings eased and it became more like gently brushing a speck of lint from my jacket. The old anchors in my life no longer held sway over me. Actually, what really changed was that I realized they *never* had power over me.

Something happens in your soul when you fully commit yourself to living your life's purpose. People and circumstances may get a bit disgruntled at first, but eventually they realize that you are serious and your soul is not to be denied. The next thing you notice when you have an unwavering commitment to your fullest revelation is that the universe embraces your good. You find that your life really is a sacred journey with a holy destination, but the destination is not out there somewhere. The destination is finding home unto yourself. The destination is finding home within yourself, in every moment, every day. Then you are living a great journey, and a great destination.

12

Thriving Under Duress

It would be lovely to end this book with the previous chapter about allowing inspiration in your everyday life. However, life happens. Unexpected events occur. There were times when goals I had dreamt of, opportunities I had longed for, finally occurred and I was stunned to find that they did not come with a rolled out red carpet and a ten-piece marching band clearing my schedule and offering up long, luxurious spaces in which to properly prepare for my highly desired opportunity.

Thoroughness dictates that we explore one last angle of inspiration: how do you allow inspiration in when the car breaks down on the way to the big job, when childcare flakes, when natural disasters foil your plans? How can you stay in the present moment, convicted in your knowing that your good is here for you, and no one and nothing can block it? More than that, how can you develop a faith and trust that your life is here for you? It is always arranged for your ultimate, highest good.

Before I got pregnant, I decided to become a doula, a birth coach who helps women through their pregnancy and the delivery of their child. The academic in me became a doula because I like knowing things before I do them. I needed to study pregnancy. I needed to see some deliveries before attempting my own. For weeks, I studied and practiced all of the vital information and techniques so that I could best assist new mothers. I went on to assist over thirty births and I would like to take this opportunity to publicly apologize to each one of those brave mothers, most of whom had signed on with me because of my "hypno-birthing" specialty.

As a licensed clinical hypnotherapist, I am well skilled in the art of directing the subconscious mind and I was quite eager to apply it in the birthing process. Gratefully, each birth I attended brought forth a healthy child. Most were the medication-free, natural child-births that the mothers had desired. However, now that I have been pregnant and know what it feels like, I must apologize to those mothers. I now know what it feels like to enter the home stretch of a ten month pregnancy marathon tired, worn out, fed up, achy, itchy, and uncomfortable. I know how it feels to then be expected to kick into high gear not just for the actual birth, but for the days, weeks, months, and years of sleep deprivation that generally accompany childbirth.

Before all of that, I could not possibly understand what those pregnant mothers were really going through. Perhaps my lack of a birthing experience actually made me more effective because I was able to hold for each new mother a conviction of healthy, successful, doable childbirth. But certainly, I did not know what it was to face the biggest moment of life weak, tired, sleep deprived, and utterly burnt out. I do now.

The feeling of being completely at the end of my rope, and yet expected to rise up and thrive full tilt, is a feeling I have come to know quite well. I always thought that moments of greatness were born in ideal circumstances. The athlete trains a regular daily practice schedule, gets a full night's sleep, then wakes comfortably and with ample time makes it to the big track meet. The actress learns lines, attends rehearsals, eats well, rests well, and then shows up to the set with time to dress and leisurely run lines. The successful business person gets the right education, does rounds of interviews, lands the starter job, and then works his way up the corporate ladder. I have come to realize that it may appear this way as we view another's successes from the outside. What is not accounted for is what happens when the athlete's bank account is empty and he still has a family to feed and a race to run. What happens when the actress' partner walks out of the marriage on opening night, or the successful businessman has a special needs child to tend to nightly and big deals to negotiate daily?

Life is not neat. It is not cleanly packaged and tied off with a lovely bow. It can be muddy and convoluted and in its own organic way, it is perfect still. How empowering to view all of it, the mistakes, poor timing, anything that feels in the moment undesirable; how empowering to make a decision that while you may wish things were different, you can declare a trust and a faith in the universe and know that beyond this veil, there is something here for your soul's highest good, greatest unfoldment on earth at this time. For years I teased my husband that the last chapter of my book would be entitled, "Thriving Under Duress." Here we are, coming to this journey's end, and truly, it is time to look at how to stay fresh and inspired when it feels like the whole world is orchestrating itself to screw you up or slow you down.

The good news is that you know something now. You can rest and trust in the fact that inspiration is a part of your human, syntropic impulse. You were born with an innate impulse to strive toward fulfillment, come what may. Truly, come what may. The dream guy leaves, the loved one passes, the parent that was not supposed to get sick, does. The job you knew was yours slips away, the time for the career, lover, life, or waist size that you know you were meant to have feels galaxies away. But now you have universal laws and principles to lean on and have faith in. You have tools to cling to through life's inevitable storms.

Michael Bernard Beckwith describes it this way: He says that your life is a set up. The experiences you encounter are a set up for your greatest growth, expansion, and transformation in this lifetime. Often times we face things that feel like setbacks, but imagine how empowering it would be to face everything that comes your way as an opportunity, an initiation, a powerful set up that causes you to rise into more of yourself.

Consider that not only is your life a set up for your ultimate greatness, but you, yourself, are the set up. The real set up is that you are the set up. Your presence is a set up for everywhere you go, everything you do, and everyone you meet. What if you decided to let your presence set up the people around you for greater joy, happiness, prosperity, fun, compassion, and kindness? This is the meaning of spiritual practice; deciding to be a deposit center. Decide that you will infuse every place you go with your uniquely designed brand of inspiration. Take a moment to consider the main qualities about yourself that you are here to embody. Now imagine what your life would be like if you made it your spiritual practice to deposit those qualities everywhere you go.

Grateful to stop in this moment. Taking in a full deep breath, easily releasing out on the exhale anything that no longer serves you. Now, see, sense, visualize yourself as a deposit center. Imagine scrolling through a day in your life and notice that everywhere you go you gift all of those around you with your presence. You are the gift. What is your gift? What qualities do you have to share and shine? If there is a color, sound, smell, shape, size to the quality of your good, notice what it is. Once again, imagine yourself moving through a day in your life leaving a trail of brilliance everywhere you go. Fill yourself with gratitude for the gifts you have been given, knowing that gratitude grows and that the more you are grateful for what you have, the more you will have to be grateful for.

I am reminded of my ashram days where I met a yogi named Heartman. He had a massive tangle of long red hair, and every day he walked around the ashram leaving little cut out hearts and love notes. That was his spiritual practice. He decided he would be "Heartman" and every day he would share love and kindness. You can find your own way to honor yourself and your purpose in this world. When you schedule in reminders to shine and share your unique qualities you will experience a true sense of satisfaction and fulfillment and you will be doing your part in leaving the world better than you found it. You can do this in the easy times and you can choose to take on the practice of staying true to who you really are no matter what unexpected events occur. The opportunity is to keep your focus on being a set up for greatness. Doing so redirects the universe when you feel off course and paves the way for more good than you ever imagined possible.

You are born of inspiration. You are born to be inspiration, illumination, joy, greatness, and brilliance. The nature of life is that it will test you and challenge you, but brilliance is your destiny and it is yours, still, when life seems to veer off point. I was offered the speaking opportunity of a lifetime after my husband began serving in Afghanistan for several months. I wanted to yell out to the universe, *How dare you call me now? How dare you wait to dangle something so delicious in front of me until a time when I am stressed beyond belief and feel I can barely function? How dare you offer me my dream job when I have no childcare to properly prepare for the opportunity or time to put together a great outfit?* Yet somehow, some way, it came together. I managed to arrange childcare. I managed to get a talk together. I even managed to take a shower and look presentable. Somehow, we are able to rise to the occasions of our life.

What's Your What?

The cliché is true; God gives us what we can handle. As a therapist, I have counseled people who lived through unimaginable circumstances. There have been times I heard someone's story and literally wanted to tell them to throw in the towel because it seemed too much for anyone to endure. Yet, I have been amazed by how these courageous individuals were able to walk, sometimes limp, step by conscious step, through their own wilderness and eventually make it back out to sunlight and possibility. Why? Because life is for you. Your life is for you. Your good is for you. No matter where you have been and what you have been through. Ultimately, your life is for you. It is for the best of you. The Creator did not breathe breath into you for normalcy or mediocrity. You were not brought forth just to go along to get along, or clock in and clock out. You are here for brilliance, for creation, for great love, for activism, and humanitarianism. You are here to right wrongs and rise up. You are here to be brave, test yourself, stretch yourself, and be so fully well spent at the end of your days that your presence has made a mighty difference on our planet and you have done your part in spiraling humanity forward. No matter what befalls you, know that your heart is renewable. Yes, we grieve our losses and lick our wounds, and then, in time, we rise again.

13

Glory Bound.
No Matter What

How good it is to have a plethora of tools readily available to ignite your own indwelling inspiration. The truth is, however, in the end you really do not need to work all that hard. Living an inspired life, bringing your innate gifts, skills, talents, and abilities into their fruition need not be laborious. It is about situating yourself in flow. It is about directing and redirecting yourself back into your life's natural flow stream.

At the beginning of 2013, Michael Bernard Beckwith spoke at Agape and said it was time to commit to being a new you in the New Year. Then he joked, "If you do not want to be new, this is not the place for you." When I heard that, I got nervous. I did not want to get kicked out of my workplace, but like so many people who are committed to a spiritual journey, I have already been growing and changing so much. I did not know what else I could possibly do to be new. I had finally joined Facebook, wasn't that enough? Then all of a sudden the word "sweetener" popped into my head and I thought, *Perfect. That is what I will do to be new this year. I am getting myself a sweetener!*

I learned about sweeteners awhile back through a circuitous route. As a teenager growing up in the South I had a disease. I suffered from good-at-everything-great-at-nothing-itis. My school even gave me an award for it, the Best All Around award. I think it was meant as a compliment, but to me it only highlighted the fact that I had no passion, no conviction. I was a who without a what, wondering why? Why am I here? What am I here for? What's my what? Ever wondered about that? What am I here for?

Dr. King said that if we do not have something we are willing to die for, we are not fit for living. This concerned me because I did not have anything, and I wanted a thing. I wanted something to go for, to be about. I wanted to know what it was like to give myself over, utterly, to a passion or conviction. I was desperate to know, "What's my what?"

Because I so lacked a what, I surrounded myself with people who had a what. As a teen, I was magnetically drawn to fellow classmates who had the kind of conviction that I craved. I also role-modeled people in the public eye who exemplified a high level of devotion and sense of purpose. One of the people I was fascinated with was Al Pacino, the great actor. I was drawn to him for two reasons. First, I admired that he knew his purpose from an early age. Second, I was fixated on him because I was raised to be a good, sweet, never-make-waves type of girl when deep down inside I wanted to live raw and guttural and passionate like Al Pacino! So I watched his films, read his biographies, and prayed that by the power of osmosis one day I would find out why I am here and then give myself over to it completely the way he gave himself over to his acting.

Given my fixation with him, you can imagine my surprise and delight when shortly after moving to New York City, I found myself working with Al Pacino! My life had hand delivered to me, with no effort or pursuit on my end, the perfect silver platter opportunity to role model the kind of passion that I craved in an up-close and star-studded kind of way. It was while I was working with Al that I learned about sweeteners.

One day we were all gathered around the conference table in his apartment as usual, but this time there was a new face at the table. I came to find out that this person was Al's sweetener. A sweetener is a professional writer, someone who comes in and tweaks dialogue, tailors an actor's words in a film to better suit the actor, and propel his character's storyline forward.

Wouldn't it be great to have a sweetener, someone to come in and tweak your day-to-day dialogue, the dialogue that you have with others and the dialogue you have with yourself? Wouldn't it be so wonderful to have someone raise the level of your conversation so that it fits you better as you are now? We grow, we change, we make new decisions, establish new convictions, beliefs, and ways of being. We need to make sure we are talking a talk that matches our ever-evolving walk, yes? Yes!

Here is a good humiliating example of how sweeteners work: I used to head up a large group of people. One day I was speaking with another person who also used to head up a large group of people. We were talking about a third person who was about to start heading up a large group of people. For our purposes I will be person 'A,' the person I was speaking with will be person 'B,' and the person we were speaking about will be person 'C.' One day, B and I were talking about C. Now, I know we were both thinking the exact same thing. We both had the same back story, facts, and figures on C, and I know we both knew the level of C's capabilities. I, however, made the unfortunate choice to speak it out loud. "Wow, C is going down. C's whole thing is going to tank. C is so grossly under qualified. This is like watching the Titanic sink in slow-motion. It is like, Titanic-Iceberg, Titanic-Iceberg, Titanic-Iceberg, Crash! Duh."

That was my good contribution to the conversation. B, who knew what I knew about C's abilities, then schooled me by saying: "Hmmm, what a tremendous opportunity we have here. I am so excited for C. This is an extraordinary moment for C to rise up beyond anything he has ever done before or even thought he could do. How thrilling is this time, how ripe is the potential of this moment." Then B turned to me and said, "And how exceptional for us; this is our chance to walk our talk, to put our spiritual practice into practice. We get to let ourselves know the very best of C in such a powerful dynamic way that he becomes triumphant beyond anything we, and even he, could ever have imagined. This is our chance to use our thoughts and convictions to elevate C into his full greatness. We get to create a vortex of excellence so compelling that our consciousness about him actually sucks him up to meet us at the level of greatness we now hold for him. How great is this moment. How powerful this time!!!" I listened to all that, and then said, "Oh, uh, yeah. That's what I meant!"

In this case, B was my sweetener. B tweaked my internal dialogue and reminded me to stay in upstairs consciousness as Dr. Homer Johnson used to say. B reminded me to raise my thoughts high, leaving room for both myself and those around me to rise up into our full divinity. Guess what? In the end, C did a good job. C did a very good job, and C will continue doing better and better every year, as long as he continues to surround himself with people who are willing to use their consciousness as support rather than hindrance, and as long as he does the same for himself. Your thoughts can either be the great big iceberg that gets crashed up against or the strong captain at the helm, guiding you through rough waters and charting your course toward new and glorious horizons.

You want to surround yourself with sweeteners, people who see your life's events in a clear, positive way. You also want to practice being your own best sweetener. The more you practice using effective language, the more reflexive positivity becomes. It is like building muscles. When you practice these sweetening skills in the simple dailiness of life, then when more challenging situations arise, you are internally fortified with the skill set necessary to maneuver yourself through all of the ins and outs of your life's adventure.

Why does attending to your thoughts and words make such a differ-ence? Dr. Masaru Emoto's well-known studies illustrate the impact of human consciousness on the molecular structure of water. This information should be especially interesting to you, given that the adult human body is comprised of approximately 60% water (Jack-son, Sheila (1985). *Anatomy & Physiology for Nurses*. Nurses' Aide Series (9th ed.). London: Bailliere Tindall) and our brain is about 80% water (McIlwain, H. and Bachelard, H.S., *Biochemistry and the Central Nervous System*, Edinburgh: Churchill Livingstone, 1985).

Dr. Emoto's experiments demonstrate that human consciousness has a direct impact on the crystalline structure of water. For ex-ample, water derived from a pristine lake or mountain river will produce a beautiful crystalline structure (when frozen) as opposed to tap water from a municipal source. Since consciousness impacts water, and your body is mostly made up of water, it makes good sense to be mindful of your thoughts.

It is time for conscious content; time to drive your thoughts with volition and intention. After the dialogue I had with B about C, clearly, I knew that I could use a good sweetener to help clean up my communications. When you do this, when you practice mindful, conscious speaking, your body, mind, and life experiences respond accordingly. You want to practice being your own best sweetener so that when you hit a bump in your life's journey, it will be there for you when you need it.

This year, I needed it. I had a familiar story. I went in for a routine check up and the doctor, using her most un-alarming voice, which of course only made her news more concerning, invited me to leave the examination room and go into her office so we could "talk." There, she told me that I had some "odd" cells which could be the big C, cancer. That meeting set off a whole flurry of doctor visits, biopsies, tests, more tests, and more doctor visits.

I went to get a second opinion from a specialist, which was really a third opinion because that doctor had already sent all of my labs and images on to her specialist. Therefore, I got the specialist's opinion and the specialist's specialist's opinion, and both agreed that I needed to have surgery and needed to do it as soon as possible. A surgery date was scheduled ten days from that appointment. Since I had ten days and a lot of tenacity, I decided to get one more opinion. I figured I would keep getting opinions until I got one I liked!

Ten days until surgery, three days until I could get in for a fourth doctor opinion. During those three days, I had my "come to Jesus moment." We have all had one, that moment that drops you to your knees. You beg God, promise everything. Here is how I did my come to Jesus moment. The exquisite singer, Charles Holt, had just performed at Agape and I had his new CD fresh and ready to go in my car stereo. I listened to that CD over and over again in my car, nonstop, blaringly loud for three days. I listened, but only to one song: "I Forgive Me." If you had passed me on the Los Angeles freeways during those three days, you would have seen me full tilt in the ugly cry, tears streaming, snot dripping. I was talking up a storm to myself, forgiving myself and everyone else, for everything. I went to town on forgiveness. I was making darn sure that I cleaned up and cleared up every moment in my life so that on the third day I could breeze into my fourth doctor's opinion and have her tell me all was well.

Have you ever been there? Ever been so driven to your knees? Dear God, please just make him call, get her to come back, let them be safe, let me be well, land the role, get the job, have the check clear, whatever it is, that moment when you are finally ready to do whatever it takes to get what you want.

I forgave every person who had ever harmed me. I listed them alphabetically, chronologically, you name it. I enumerated all of their offenses and forgave every last one of them. Then I woke up the next day and forgave myself, for not really forgiving every *last* one of them. I forgave myself for having people in my life that I did not like. Then I did the work until I could see and feel their goodness and know that love is their true nature. I stayed with it until I could feel this truth in a clear and authentic way, and then I forgave myself for waking up the next day and still not really liking them all that much.

I forgave myself for failing at forgiveness. I forgave myself for spending hundreds, probably thousands of dollars in my life try-ing to get over hurts I experienced early on in life, and I forgave myself for still harboring areas that hold the residue of pain and un-forgiveness. I forgave myself for all of the times I have hurt others, the people from whom I have withheld love, forgiveness, time, acceptance, or energy.

What's Your What?

I forgave myself for every time I sent my child off to school without an excellent home-cooked breakfast. Then I forgave myself for every time I sent my son to school with an awesome steel-cut-oatmeal-goji-eating-greens-infused breakfast, but then I screwed up something else because no matter how hard I try to get it all right all the time, I am not perfect and something always seems to slide. I forgave myself for my imperfections.

I forgave myself for showing up month after month to the Leadership Meetings without a home baked pie because I am from the South and you are supposed to bring baked goods when you go places, but Michael Beckwith only eats vegan food and all my attempts at vegan cooking end up tasting like cardboard. I forgave myself for making my poor kid leave out cardboard-tasting vegan cookies last Christmas for Santa Claus. Brick-like vegan cookies and warm almond milk, do you have any idea how disappointed Santa must have been when he got to our house? It is no wonder that my son did not get the brand new iPad he asked for!

I forgave myself for every ant I had ever stepped on in the entire course of my life, and then I forgave myself for even thinking I should forgive myself for stepping on ants because ants are really, really small and it would be very hard to go through an entire life without ever stepping on one. I forgave and cleansed and cried and purified and begged for three solid days. I had Charles Holt's voice forgiving me in the car during the days, and then to max the whole thing out, I had Tim Mcafee-Lewis's version of "I Forgive Me" slay me on my home stereo during the nights.

By the time I went in for my fourth doctor's opinion, I was drained, exhausted, and close to surrender. The doctor examined me, checked my labs, and then said, "Hmm, I don't see why we need to slice you open just yet. Why don't we do a dye test and then if we have to move forward we will." *Dye test? What the heck is a dye test?* I thought, and why the heck was that the first time I was hearing of this nonsurgical easy-peasy option?! What a profoundly clear reminder that we really do need to be our own advocates when it comes to health. Turns out, they could shoot some dye inside of me and if it does one thing, it is time to sharpen the scalpels, but if it does another thing that just means those "odd" cells are a unique part of my internal topography and I am close to off the hook. The dye test sounded like a great option, but then I remembered I was scheduled for surgery in seven days so I asked how soon I could get the dye test and how long it would take to get the results. "Right now and five minutes," said the doctor, so off we went.

During the five minutes that I waited to find out the dye test result, I had my second, more amped up, come to Jesus moment. As I waited in the cold, sterile examination room, I begged God. I cajoled. I argued. I bargained, "*If you get me through this, I will do better. I will love more. I will give more. I will serve more. I'll figure out this whole forgiveness thing more.*" *I tried to make God feel guilty.* 'You cannot mess with me. I am a mother. I have a young child that needs me. My husband will raise him on eggnog and salami if I am not around. I have to be here to raise my kid.* I was so deeply lost in my own drama, tears streaming down my face, lips mouthing my admonishments to God, that I did not even hear the first throat clearing. It was probably the third or fourth time before

I realized that the doctor was back in the room and trying to get my attention. Apparently, she had walked in while I was having my own private soap opera. "No need for slicing and dicing yet," she told me. The dye test came out negative, which is positive.

My first thought was to send nasty-grams to all of the other doctors I had been to for not even mentioning a dye test option, but then, realizing that I was not yet out of the woods, I immediately forgave myself for thinking nasty-gram thoughts. The last step, the doctor said, was two more biopsies in areas we had not yet covered. Seven days until my surgery date. Five days for biopsy results. If they come back clear, then bye bye surgery.

Something happened during those five days while I was waiting for the biopsy results. I let go. I had not planned to, and perhaps it was simply the sheer exhaustion from wrenching myself of all energy and emotion during the days prior, but suddenly I felt peaceful. Extremely peaceful. Euphorically peaceful. I felt, "the peace that passes human understanding." People talk about it all the time; they are always praying that so-and-so has the peace that passes human understanding. I felt it! I was so psyched!

Then the extraordinary occurred. During those five days, on two separate occasions, for about a millisecond each time, I had the genuine awareness that all is well. Even if the tests did not go my way, even if that meant not reaching my personal goals in this lifetime. Even if it meant leaving my son with his dad and not being around to make sure my boy wears a jacket on chilly days, on two separate occasions, for about a millisecond each time, I had the sublimely peaceful realization that all is well and all will continue to be well, even if I was not.

On the fifth day, I received a call from the doctor letting me know that the tests had come back negative, which is positive, and finally I could close the chapter on that whole crazy episode in my life. Now it is time for the sweetener. Have you ever made it through one of life's windstorms and then finally had a moment to reflect on what the heck that was all about? Here is the good news; you get to decide. If a tree falls in the woods and no one is around to hear it fall, did it make a noise? Depends on what you decide. If you decide it did, then it did. If you decide it did not, then it did not. The only reality that exists is the one that we create because there is no such thing as "real" reality. Reality is expressed after moving through your subjective, human filtering system. This is why two people can grow up in the same household and have completely different memories of their home life. So, since you are making it all up anyway, why not make it hot? Why not make choices and decisions about your life experiences that raise you up, make you better, make you stronger, let you be happier?

I once had a client who had been through the worst of the worst. I heard her story, and even for me as the trained professional, I wanted to tell her to throw in the towel. I saw no way to recover from what she had been through, but extraordinarily enough, she told me that while she was in the dramatic situation she recalled making a decision that the experience would have her for the moment, but it would not have her for the rest of her life. We are the ones who attribute meaning and value to the circumstances of our lives. This is where your sweetener comes in.

What's Your What?

It would have been so easy for me to be bitter, to spend the next days, weeks, months, years of my life ranting about my negative sojourn in western medicine. How many times have we done that? Let ourselves get derailed with energy-draining bitterness or resentments. This is why you need a strong, reflexive sweetener. My sweetener jumped right in to remind me of those two milliseconds of true faith. My sweetener reminded me that I could not pay enough money for the realization that now lives in my soul. I have felt a kind of peace that I never knew was possible. The peace that passes human understanding that people quote from scripture, I know what that is. I have felt it, and in my line of work as a minister, that is a pretty clutch awareness to have! I could put that on my resume:

Reverend Julie Moret

Employment

- Speaker, Agape International Spiritual Center

Education

- Agape University of Transformational Studies & Leadership

Skills and Hobbies

- Public Speaking

- Yoga

- Knows the peace that passes human understanding!

Julie Moret

I have had two milliseconds of knowing what it is to be truly free. I now know that real faith, real trust, and real surrender are all possible. That was my gift. In every moment, you have the power to reframe your experiences in a way that gives your life wings.

This is the point—you are powerful beyond measure. Yes, we stay in gratitude for modern medical technology. Yes, we are absolutely responsible for caring for our bodies and pursuing diagnosis and clarity. *And*, we stay mindful that we are more than this. We are more than test results and statistics. We stay mindful that we are choosing; we are choosing a heart-centered, faith-based, conscious life. We know that first and foremost, no matter what western medical practices we employ, we let prayers be our scalpels and thoughts be our pharmaceuticals. This is how you make your life a birthing field for miracles.

That is the first part—becoming your own best sweetener. Sometimes, however, it takes more than shifting or adjusting the dialogue of your life. Sometimes the words we use and the talk we talk simply will not do. What happens when you cannot paint a pretty face on a situation, wrap a bow around it and move on? When this happens, when the sweetener does not sweeten, then it is time for all new words, and a whole new language to boot. This year, I needed a new language.

About a year ago, I woke up one day feeling pregnant. I just felt pregnant. I felt like I was supposed to be pregnant. So I turned to my husband and said, "I think I am supposed to be pregnant." I then had the spousal pleasure of watching smoke unfurl from my

- 152 -

husband's ears as his brain short circuited. You see, after we had our child, my husband and I sat down and had a very practical, realistic, rational conversation. We made a verbally and orally-binding agreement whereby we clearly determined that we were happy with our one child and that we were done. As they say, "one and done." A friend had once said to us, "one good one is all you need," and that became our creed. We arranged our living situation, finances, career goals, and all major life choices on the basis that we were one and done. So, I watched my well-organized, major- planner, husband's brain go haywire as I whimsically mentioned that I felt I was supposed to get pregnant. It took a moment, but he easily jumped on board and off we went on our new quest.

The small hitch in this plan is that we both have fast-paced, regularly-traveling lifestyles, so each month when that special time came around to actually get pregnant, we simply were not in the same place at the same time to get the job done, so to speak. No matter, I got pregnant anyway. Not physically pregnant, psychologically pregnant. My husband and I would be sitting on the couch and I would try to stand up, one hand on my belly, the other hand heaving me up. I waddled in and out of the various rooms of my life. I was not doing a fake-it-till-you-make-it kind of a deal. I do understand what is required for conception; I just felt pregnant. I am not talking about a cute, little, first trimester baby bump type thing. I felt grossly, massively pregnant, like end-of-third-trimester-with-quadruplets-ready-to-drop-my-load-at-any-second, pregnant!

This behavior went on for months. One day my husband came home from work to find me sitting on the living room couch, zoned out on TV with a vat of ice cream in my lap. I could hear his breath catch, knew he wanted to say something, but realized he was trying to be considerate given my fragile, psychologically-pregnant state. As he crossed the room to put his things down, I imagined him reciting a mantra to himself over and over again in order to keep his cool: *She's crazy. I know that she's crazy. I knew that she was crazy when I married her, but she's my kind of crazy. She's crazy. I know that she's crazy. I knew that she was crazy when I married her, but she's my kind of crazy...*

As he walked back across the room toward the kitchen, I could see him still doing his best not to pay attention to my bizarre behavior. He was probably thinking, *I know she's really into her mind and consciousness and stuff. Maybe she thinks if she gains thirty pounds of fat, it will turn into a kid. I don't know...* Just as he was about to make it into the kitchen, I spooned out another huge scoop of ice cream and that was it, he could not keep it in any more. "You are not pregnant! What are you doing?" he exploded at me. No matter, he did not offend me one bit. I knew that my psychologically-pregnant self had psychological hormones running amuck, so I simply glared at him, shoved the spoon back in my trough, and went right back to watching television!

I finally hit rock bottom the day I showed up for services wearing a fetching, brown potato sack. At that point, it was the only thing that I felt I could get around my ever imaginarily expanding girth, which at this point was not so imaginary. I looked like I had gone into a cheap motel, taken one of their curtains off of the window, and swathed it ever so elegantly around my body. Right before Rev.

What's Your What?

Michael walked up on stage he came over to me, looked at my outfit, and said, "Huh...did you make that?" Here is one little tip: It is never a good thing when your boss asks if you made your outfit! Unless you are a fabulous fashion designer, it is not a good thing. Finally, I realized this whole psychologically-pregnant situation was out of hand.

We have all been there. Well, maybe you have not been psychologically pregnant, but certainly you know what it is to want something so dearly, something you would give everything for. And then it finally happened. At last, I was really pregnant. I was pregnant and we were elated. Then I got the speaking opportunity of a lifetime. Things were just getting better and better. I was up on stage speaking all day long, fulfilling my greatest dreams, playing at the level I know I was meant to play at, and I had a miscarriage. There was no kind of sweetener, no way no how that could make that situation better. I was not interested in any tidy, little life lessons or positive reframes.

The only thing I did notice, however, when I finally got home at the end of that long, wonderful horrible day, was a slight glimmer of awareness that drifted through my consciousness as I climbed upstairs to my bedroom, drew the curtains tightly closed, and let the blackness envelope me. After sinking down into my bed and into a pretty deep depression, a brief awareness flickered across my mind. It occurred to me that when I woke up a year earlier feeling pregnant, I really was pregnant. I had been happy with my one and done child but figured that the powerful pregnant feeling meant I was supposed to have another child, and I grew to want to have another child. I wanted the kind of pregnancy that results in ten fingers, ten toes, and projectile poops. What I finally realized on that day, buried under mounds of blankets and shrouded in darkness, was that I had been pregnant all along.

You see, I had spoken several times that day. Each time when I finished speaking, I was inundated with opportunities. It was so overt:

"I want to write a book with you."

"I want to give you a book deal."

"Would you like to be a specialty guest on a talk show?"

"I produce talk shows, would you like your own talk show?"

"Want to be on a reality show?"

"Ever thought about soap operas?"

"Can I book you as a speaker for my next conference?"

"I own a resort in the islands; can I fly you down to speak there?"

"Will you be a guest on my radio show?"

"Would you like your own radio show?"

On and on it went all day long. I received such a glut of opportunities, I was birthing dreams I had set in motion most of my life. This realization passed over me briefly, like a blink, and then was gone along with my heart and my hopes for quite some time as I mourned the loss of my baby. When I finally drew back the curtains and let the sun shine through once again, I decided it was time to speak a new language. I could not sweeten this situation, was not interested in tweaking my dialogue so I could put a happy face on it. What I could do, however, was turn the page. That is really the point, knowing when to say when. I realized that for a year I had blinders on. All I could see or think about was getting pregnant. Baby talk was my only language. I decided, finally, for my health, for my peace of mind, I needed to speak a new language.

It is not that wanting a baby was wrong or that I misinterpreted what the feeling of being pregnant meant, it was simply that the road on which I had been traveling seemed blocked at every turn and it was time to harmonize with the areas in my life where there was flow, massive flow. This kind of flexibility is vital in our lives. Ultimately, it is about knowing when to say when. You see, sometimes we get to choose when to change gears, and sometimes the choice is made for us. Sometimes, the person that is supposed to love someone forever and ever wakes up one day and decides they are just not that into them anymore. Sometimes, the once in a lifetime marriage does not last the lifetime. Sometimes, someone dies who was not supposed to, according to you and your heart. Sometimes, the medical test comes back positive, which does not feel so positive. In this case, when the sweetener does not sweeten, when you cannot reshape or put a spin on your current words, then it is time to find all new words, and a whole new language to boot!

How many people have you known that faced a hard time and let themselves get derailed by it for the next several years, or decades, or even the rest of their life? Given some of the things I have been through, I could understand that. I could understand that if we were here to get by as unscathed as possible. I could understand that, if we were here to make it from the top of each day to the bottom, nice and tight and safe; if we were merely here to clock in and clock out every day. Wake up, eat something, do something, watch something, go to bed. Wake up, eat something, do something, watch something, go to bed. But we are more than this. You are more than this.

You are here for a life. It is not a life sentence. It is a life and it is the only one you've got. Well, let me clarify. Yes, we probably have many lifetimes. We come back over and over again to grow and evolve in consciousness, but nothing is guaranteed. You may be coming back next time around as a frog, nothing against frogs, so you want to get your life right this time around. Get it while it is hot. Get it while you are hot!

You are meant for greatness. You are meant for glory. Imagine looking yourself in the mirror each morning and brightly declaring, "I am bound for glory!" At first your reflection in the mirror will probably say, "Huh? I thought we were bound for Starbucks." But soon, with your spiritual practice in place, with conviction and willingness in your heart, you will come to expect and demand for yourself a broad, self-inspired life lived in great big strokes with brilliant colors. Somewhere along the line, we received misinformation. We thought we were here to get by without any scratches, but this is incorrect. You are here for an adventure. You are here on the hero's journey, and you are the hero. You are the hero you have been waiting for.

Yes, you will have bumps in the road. Yes, you will have moments that drop you to your knees, but then you rise again. There are dragons to slay, mountains to climb, great and mighty battles to wage. If you are not literally picking up the sword in this lifetime, perhaps you are dueling with your ego, soaring in love, challenging yourself in your ability to forgive or serve or care or share. You may be here to rescue true principles from false thinking like a damsel in distress. You are the hero of your own journey. You have the tools to self-actualize. You hold the keys to regularly inspiring your life, flooding it with passion and purpose.

You did not come here to mark time. You came into this life with inspiration coursing through your veins, electrically surging in your thoughts, stamped like a passport on your very DNA. You have come into this life preprogrammed for glory. When you allow this, when you say yes to your good, when you get your tools in place and sweeten your thoughts, words, and deeds in the simple dailiness of life, when you have the fortitude and willingness to switch gears and move newly as need be, when need be, then, you could not write the wonders that await you. You could not dream them.

I could never have imagined the adventures that awaited me when I was a teen growing up in the South, being raised to be a sweet, dainty, little wallflower while some version of Al Pacino's character in Scarface raged inside of me. I could never have imagined that one day I would dance the tango with Al Pacino at his Academy Awards party after he won. I could never fathom that I would casually hang out at Al's country house reading through Othello with Al Pacino, Kevin Spacey, Estelle Parsons, and F. Murray Abraham. I could not have written that script, couldn't have dreamt it.

Then, at last, I got mine. I found my what. This all began with a child's deep, earnest longing, *Lord, why am I here? What am I here for? What do you want of me? What's my what? Give me a clue.* Finally, I started getting clues. While I was working with Al, I took up a couple of side hobbies. I attended Eric Butterworth's talks at Lincoln Center. I enrolled in the Barbara Brennan School of Healing where we studied hands-on energy healing. Finally, I was around people who spoke my language. It was a language I had never heard before, never been taught, but boy did I understand it. No translator needed.

Then one day while I was away studying at the healing school, I received a call from Al Pacino's office asking me to come to a big event. In the past, I would have dropped everything and shown up for the occasion, no questions asked. But this time I did not want to leave. I was seeing angels and running energy through my hands and incredibly enough I was surrounded by fellow students who were doing the same thing! Some dormant part of me was waking up, and I finally had a safe home to find and express myself. I could not leave. No more leaving. No more abandoning who I really am for who I think I should be. My ego was not on the same page. It was having a full-on temper tantrum trying to get me to go, but my soul was finally at home unto itself and I could not be moved. I did not move. I did not go back.

What's Your What?

Shortly thereafter, I took a trip to Los Angeles and visited the Agape International Spiritual Center. When I walked in, my life felt like it was no longer housing an alien. I found home within and life began anew. I met and married a man who makes my life better, accepts and supports my laser-like passion, and knows that I am crazy but welcomes me as his kind of crazy. We have a child who floods our life with joy, humor, and energy. All of this good coupled with the fact that I get to travel and speak to thousands of people all around the world. I could never have imagined that I would find myself in such a congruent, inspired life. I could not have dreamt it, but you can expect it. You can expect your good. Why? Because you are bound for glory. Because you are built from inspiration. It is a guide flowing through you like a river ready to carry you home unto yourself if you will but let it. Truly, you are bound for glory, no matter what.

Conclusion

Darwin Was Wrong

You now know that inspiration is an innate aspect of your spiritual, physical, psychological self and that there are many ways to cultivate a relationship with your indwelling inspiration—but, to what end? Why is it so important to engage your inspiration? Because it allows you to be who you are meant to be? Yes. Because it helps you create more and enjoy your life more? Of course. Because when you do so, you are able to be more of an impactful, beneficial presence on the planet? Yes, all true. Still, why embrace your inspiration? Because it is your key to becoming unloosed.

To become unloosed means to untie yourself, remove all restraints. It means, to set yourself free. I am a woman unloosening. I am a woman becoming myself. Ironically, the I that I am becoming is the I that I have always been. I knew who I was early on. I believe that on some level, all people do. Yet like so many, I got the unsaid message early on in life that shining too bright can be dangerous. For me, the thought of claiming and living my passion aloud was akin to walking the plank or stretching my neck out across a guillotine.

Over time, I succumbed to letting the radiance of me be my best-kept secret. I would take it out and dust it off a few times a year just to remember who I really am, and then go back to my dark, quiet, solo apartment with its stacked-to-the-ceiling movie rentals, munching on popcorn with olive oil and M&Ms as I numbed out to movie after movie. It seemed almost doable to ignore the desire that burned inside of me.

Perhaps it seems almost doable to you right now. Maybe you could keep clocking in under the radar. Maybe. Maybe you can skirt by for a few months, or years, or even decades, but eventually that passion that was planted within you even before birth, eventually that knowing of who you really are, your true dynamic nature, the true need to shine and share, and guide and teach, and transform, rise up, fight back, speak out, make a difference, be the difference... eventually it demands its due. Rise to your call now. Remember, you may be coming back in the next lifetime as a frog, so you may as well get this whole human thing now while you can! Do not wait until the gentle little knocks at your conscience's door grow into great big bangs in the form of an unwanted diagnosis or sudden loss. That seed of specialness that was placed within you from the beginning never leaves. It always wants full revelation of itself through you.

What's Your What?

Nobel Prize-winning scientist Albert Szent-Gyorgyi located a biological impulse to move toward wholeness, advancement, and true perfection. This drive is the yearning of man's innate inspiration unleashing both automatically and biochemically within the self. Aristotle's teachings claim that inspiration dwells in the four humors, which are all located in the bloodstream. Numerous yogis profess the ability to access inspiration via specific breathing techniques and yogic postures. Plato believed that the poet's mind temporarily breaks through to the world of divine truth and this inspired shift in psychology allows inspiration to enter. Sigmund Freud located inspiration in the psyche, while Carl Gustav Jung's theory of inspiration is connected to racial memory of psychologically-encoded archetypes. Psychologist Mihaly Csikszentmihalyi's theory of flow mirrors many of the basic tenants of inspiration, and both Michael Bernard Beckwith and Wayne Dyer have created spiritual practices and strategies that enhance inspirational flow in daily life. All know inspiration. All claim it as available and accessible. That is the easy good news.

Now comes the part that requires sweat. It requires breath, commitment, and willingness. It requires a holy "yes." Inspiration is within. Your inspiration is within you right now. It flows in your veins. It is conveyed via built-in neurological and biological pathways as well as old archetypal imprints. Court this treasure. Clarify which facets of the diamond are yours. How are you meant to shine? What are you meant to share? Create an environment and support system that nurtures your light along with spiritual practices and disciplines that invite the holy of holies to be revealed through you on a daily basis. This is your invitation home. It has no expiration date. You can accept it now or ten years from now, this lifetime or the next. God lives beyond time. Your good is eternal.

A young man once asked God how long a million years was to Him. God said, "A million years to me is just like a single second in your time." Then the young man asked God what a million dollars was to Him. God replied, "A million dollars to me is just like a single penny to you." The young man got his courage up and asked, "God, could I have one of your pennies?" God smiled and replied, "Certainly, just a second."

I do not know who first told that story. I do know that during all of the years I spent waiting for my life to "happen" it was happening. My inspiration was simply dormant, waiting for me while I was waiting for it. The full realization of your gifts and talent is not something you beg of God and then sit back and wait to happen. The fulfillment of your good is a team effort. You can sit on the sidelines and let inspiration unexpectedly splash you in the face like a bucket of cold ice water every few months or years, or you can create a lifestyle that nourishes inspiration, that coaxes it out and lets you ride it on long waves of excellence revealed as manifested radiance.

It is time for a revolution of the psyche. It is time to inspire yourself and others. It is time to consciously change old thought and belief patterns for the purpose of greater freedom, both internally and experientially out in the world. Both brains, the one in your head and your full body brain known as your nervous system, can be jailer or freedom bearer depending on how they are used. Prayer is Creation. Thought backed by emotion, creates. Prayer spoken with conviction and certainty can move mountains, perhaps it built pyramids...

A few years ago when I was feeling especially far from my true self, I started attracting some very "in my face" type clients in my counseling practice. In one year, I had three New York Times best-selling authors, a top publisher of multiple best-selling new age inspirational books, and two Academy Award winners. All were seeking my guidance. I wanted to blurt out, *Why are you coming to me? I want to be where you are!!!* I kept trying to hide from that light inside of me and it just kept showing up bigger and louder. No place to run. No place to hide. May as well shine. Do you know that by now? Do you know that the seed of your desire will not be washed over? You may as well nurture it and let it grow. It will not be denied. You will not be denied.

What happens when a person becomes unloosed? They take actions anyway. You may feel trepidation, but you move anyway. While it may feel like each step is walking you further out along a rocky abyss, your job is to keep stepping, keep trusting even as phantoms from your past drift around you. Even when it feels like your life is trying to suck you back into your old self. You keep stepping. You grow your faith. Raise your trust. Stand more and more in the conviction of your everlasting good, and then rest in the sweet harvest. There is no lid on the bounteous possibility of your life.

Backed in this certainty, the only questions remaining are how to allow your indwelling inspiration to continuously unfold into more and more of who you really are, and how your presence can assist others in doing the same. The questions now are how far, how wide, how deep can you go in this lifetime? How immediate can the return rate be from thought to inspiration to realization and manifestation? Lastly, what kind of inspiration are you going for? Do you want a little something here and there to sprinkle a drop of happiness? Or, perhaps, you are ready to tear it up and go full tilt into that divine unrest, the continuous upward, outward, onward unfolding of who you really are.

Inspiration flows in your veins. It is an unending, unresting well-spring. It is ever reaching out to you, showing you that your highs can get higher and the fathoms of your thoughts and consciousness can go deeper. It is a blessed unrest. It is one sting. One full-tilt sting and you are out. Darwin was wrong. It is not about survival of the fittest. That is archaic patriarchal thinking. Survival of the fittest falsely perpetuates a hierarchical mentality. Hierarchy is a misnomer. It does not work. There was a time when it may have seemed like a workable model. No more. We are on a living planet that will not tolerate nonsense. All of us in all of our cities, towns, countries, and villages must use new words and new models such as cooperation, acceptance, support, service, giving, kindness, and compassion. These concepts are not wishy-washy or "lite." They are more powerful and effective long term than any military op or corporate takeover, but surviving in this new paradigm is no simple feat.

Survival is for the ones willing to break their hearts wide open and love the most. It is survival for the ones willing to trust the most, willing to give and serve, and share, and contribute the most. Survival now is for those willing to reveal their greatness and share it with the world. Are you willing now? I hope so, because anything less is just marking time. Be bold, yes? And get it while you're hot!

Blessings on the journey, Julie

References

Cornford, F. (1971). The Doctrine of Eros in Plato's Symposium. In G. Vlastos (Ed.), *A Collection of Critical Essays: Ethics, Politics and Philosophy of Art and Religion* Doubleday Anchor, 1971

Csikszentmihalyi, M. (2008). *Flow: The Psychology of Optimal Experience.* New York: Harper Perennial Modern Classics.

Frost, R. (1928). Once by the Pacific, 1928

Ghiselin, B. (1955). *The Creative Process.* New York: Mentor.

Harding, R. (1948). *An Anatomy of Inspiration.* Cambridge: W. Heffer & Sons Ltd.

Jaynes, J. (1977). *The Origin of Consciousness in the Breakdown of the Bicameral Mind.* Boston: Houghton Mifflin.

Jung, C. (1933). *Modern Man in Search of a Soul.* London: Keegan

Paul, Trench, Trubner &Co.

Jung, C. (1963). *Memories, Dreams, Reflections.* New York: Pantheon Books.

Obama, B. (2006). *The Audacity of Hope.* New York: Crown Publishers, 2006

Parini, J. (2000). *Robert Frost: A Life.* New York: Henry Holt and Company.

Rorty, R. (1980). *Philosophy and the Mirror of Nature.* Oxford: Basil Blackwell.

Szent-Gyorgyi, A. (1977). Drive in Living Matter to Perfect Itself. *Synthesis 1, 1* (1), 14-26.

Tirtha, Swami Rama. "The Nature of Inspiration." Golden Gate Hall [Speech]. San Francisco. 21 Feb. 1903

von Goethe, J. (1988). *Faust.* New York: Bantam.

Dr. Martin Luther King Jr. Why We Can't Wait. Signet Classics, 2000

Plato, C.D.C Reeve, Republic, Hackett Publishing Co. 3rd ed., 2004

The Works of Robert G. Ingersoll, Dresden Memorial Edition (II, 420), Editing by Cliff Walker

About the Author

Julie Moret earned degrees in a range of healing-specific subjects, including psychology and neurolinguistic programming. A successful personal coach and speaker who has seen her work featured on the Lifetime television channel, she enjoys working with clients from diverse backgrounds, including Fortune 500 executives, Academy Award winners, and several New York Times best-selling authors.

Julie, an Agape International Spiritual Center speaker, staff minister, and member of the Executive Leadership Board, was knighted alongside Jack Canfield, Don Miquel Ruiz, and Michael Bernard Beckwith by the Order of the Orthodox Knights of St. John Russian Grand Priory.

Visit *www.juliemoret.com* for more information.